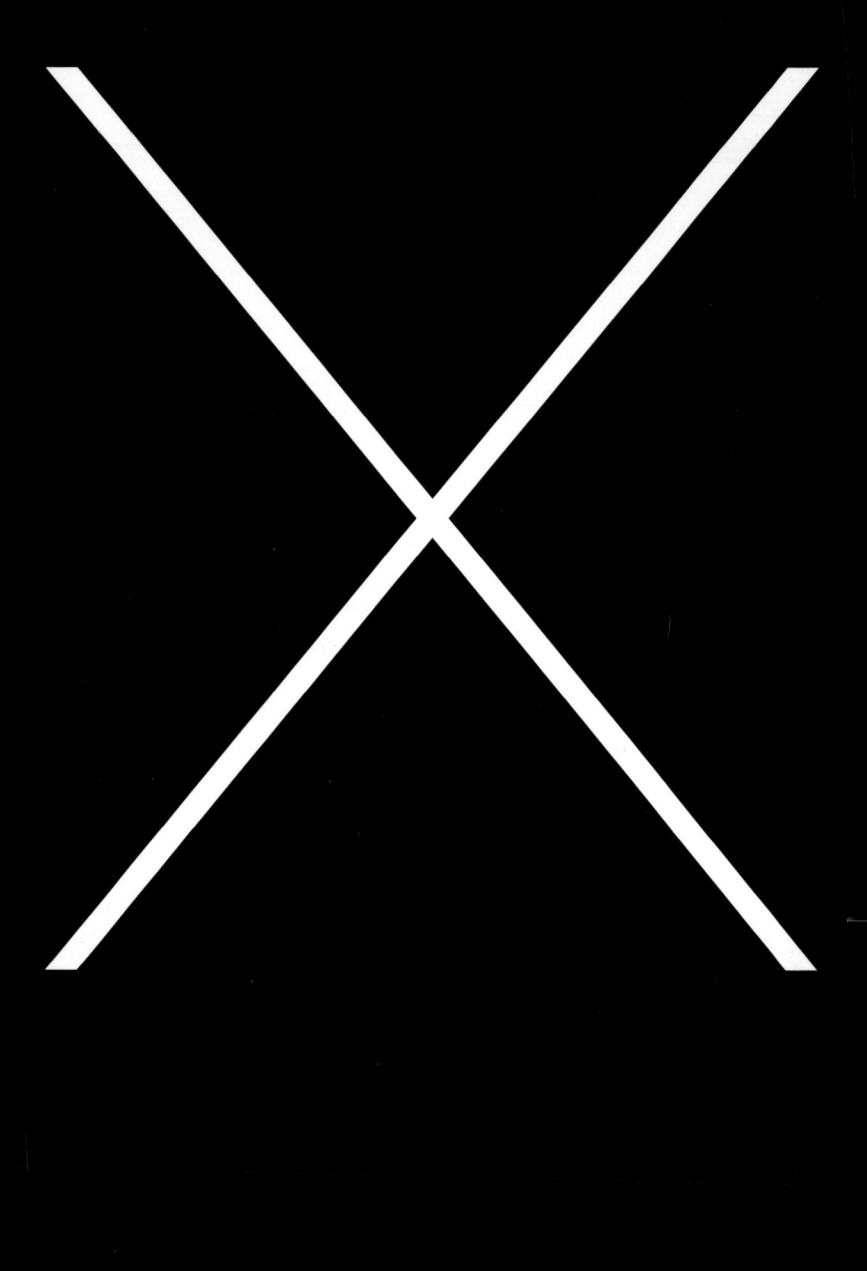

Young Architects 14
No Precedent

Foreword by R. E. Somol
Introduction by Anne Rieselbach

Bureau Spectacular
Jimenez Lai

Koji Tsutsui & Associates
MMX Studio
Jorge Arvizu
Emmanuel Ramirez
Diego Ricalde
Ignacio del Rio

SOFTlab
Michael Szivos

stpmj
Seung Teak Lee
Mi Jung Lim

WEATHERS
Sean Lally

Princeton Architectural Press
The Architectural League of New York

Published by
Princeton Architectural Press
37 East 7th Street
New York, New York 10003

www.papress.com

To view podcast interviews with each firm,
please visit the Architectural League's
website at www.archleague.org.

Editor: Dan Simon
Cover design: Pentagram
Interior layout: Benjamin English

Special thanks to:
Sara Bader, Janet Behning,
Nicola Bednarek Brower, Fannie Bushin,
Megan Carey, Carina Cha, Andrea Chlad,
Russell Fernandez, Will Foster, Jan Haux,
Diane Levinson, Jennifer Lippert,
Katharine Myers, Margaret Rogalski,
Elana Schlenker, Sara Stemen,
Andrew Stepanian, Paul Wagner,
and Joseph Weston of Princeton
Architectural Press
—Kevin C. Lippert, publisher

This publication is supported, in part,
by public funds from the New York City
Department of Cultural Affairs in partnership
with the City Council and the New York
State Council on the Arts with the support
of Governor Andrew Cuomo and the New
York State Legislature.

Library of Congress
Cataloging-in-Publication Data

Young architects 14: no precedent /
foreword by R.E. Somol; introduction by
Anne Rieselbach. — First [edition].
pages cm. — (Young architects; 14)
ISBN 978-1-61689-105-3 (pbk.)
1. Architectural League Prize for Young
Architects and Designers—Exhibitions.
2. Architecture—Awards—United States.
3. Architecture—United States—History—
21st century. 4. Young architects—United
States. I. Somol, Robert. II. Rieselbach,
Anne. III. Architectural League of New York.
NA2340.Y67995 2013
720.79'73—dc23

                            2012041867

Contents

Acknowledgments

Annabelle Selldorf, President
The Architectural League of New York

The Architectural League values the collaborative nature of design and, like most of its programs, the Architectural League Prize for Young Architects + Designers is a collaborative effort, from the call for entries to the jury, exhibition, lectures, and this catalog. No Precedent, the thirty-first annual competition, was made possible by the efforts of the League Prize Committee, competition jurors, exhibition cosponsors, program sponsors, and the staff of the Architectural League.

The portfolio competition was open to architects and designers ten years or less out of undergraduate or graduate school, with the competition theme, No Precedent, developed by the League Prize Committee, to reflect current issues in architectural design and theory. The 2011/2012 committee of Emily Abruzzo, Dominic Leong, and Michael Loverich—all past League Prize winners—spent considerable time crafting the provocative theme and text for the call for entries, and conveyed their ideas to Michael Bierut and Britt Cobb of Pentagram, who provided the competition and exhibition graphics. The committee also selected experienced members of the design community to serve with them on the jury. I was pleased to serve as a juror with them alongside Toshiko Mori, Gregg Pasquarelli, Lisa Phillips, and Robert Somol. We selected the winning entries from a strong group of well over one hundred submissions.

The competition winners created installations, gave lectures, and took part in interviews, which are provided on the League's website as podcasts. All of these, for the third year, were presented at the Sheila C. Johnson Design Center at Parsons The New School for Design. We would like to thank the Design Center staff, Radhika Subramaniam, Kristina Kaufman, and Daisy Wong, for their time and expertise. Thanks also to David Sundberg of ESTO, who once again photographed the exhibition. Anne Rieselbach, the League's program director, directs the overall League Prize program and was assisted by program associate Gabriel Silberblatt and program intern Saga Blane.

The program is made possible by the generous support of Dornbracht, Susan Grant Lewin Associates, and Tishler und Sohn. League programs are supported, in part, by public funds from the New York State Council on the Arts with the support of Governor Andrew Cuomo and the New York City Department of Cultural Affairs in partnership with the City Council.

Foreword: And Now for Something Completely Similar
R. E. Somol

When you set "No Precedent" as a theme, you can't be surprised by what you get. This is simply the way that this particular one-two punch works: the play promised by the unprecedented is immediately undercut by the conventions requisite for the establishment of a theme. Where anything is possible, everything has been seen before.

In this instance, the "what you see is what you had" experience is abetted by the jury process itself, as the League Prize is not a juror's medium, whatever the desire of individual jurors might be. The structure emphasizes continuity (the involvement of recent alumni of the award, the background legacy of the thirty-year history of recipients) and militates against the jury (a relatively large and eclectic group, given the time and task) making anything that could be interpreted as a collective statement through the six (no more, no less) finalists.

The jury is assembled, self-evidently, to pick winners. Or perhaps it would be more accurate to say that the jury is convened to *confirm* winners, since what is remarkable is how accomplished all the finalists are, and always seem to be, despite their relative youth. They have won significant awards before, and they will presumably do so again. But if a jury in this institutional context is not particularly well suited to make statements, it does rather effectively provide the social function of vetting future colleagues (something akin to a tenure process) and contributing to the grooming of careers.

Indeed, even a moderately skillful practitioner in the art of the CV can kill six sections with one submission: award, exhibition, publication, lecture, commissioned project (the installation itself, as opposed to the work exhibited), and service (the potential to participate as future committee member and juror). This is a jackpot of resume building, though one that comes with its own cautionary tale for professional practice, a lesson that will be relearned many times in one's future career: each of those activities has netted just south of $200.

While the professional merits of each of the individual finalists are beyond dispute, the relative enthusiasm that one can muster about specific projects varies wildly. For me, about half of the work presented here opens exciting disciplinary options that I would like to see exploited, while the remainder, though admirable, does not warrant a second look. I assume this breakdown more or less accords with the experience of the other jurors, though they would (and did) draw the lines differently. It would not even surprise me to learn that there might be a project that *no one* is retrospectively enthusiastic about. This has to do with the fact that, at a certain point in the deliberations, the group finds itself curating a set, and the expectation kicks in (perhaps due to fatigue or as a procedural expedient to group decision making) that the awards should represent the diversity of types of entry.

However one feels about the issue of precedent, there are certainly no more than a handful of established genres into which the one hundred–plus entries can be divided: crafty and often overly intricate installations (extra points for images of router heads or pickups hauling stacks of carefully labeled pieces of indistinguishable variety), green growie stuff (from river reclamation and would-be High Lines to window boxes and the cliché du jour urban farm), designs with people in them (extra points for images of community meetings or happy children), portfolios that recall the fine art of drawing (from old school to digital, it is the easy listening that architects never tire of seeing played out in all its virtuosity). Collectively, these constitute (and have since time immemorial) the identikit for the self-recognition of the profession: technical competence in construction, responsibility toward the environment, commitment to the community, and an excusable proclivity for the aesthetics of representation. Nothing to be ashamed of, but neither is it a particular cause for excitement.

This sociology of decision-making, which seems structural more than authored by specific juries, accounts for two impressions. The first is the serial eclecticism of the work presented, a diversity that is never quite held together by the theme, the task of which is to attempt to prospectively overcome the incongruences exhibited. The second is the sense that *any* of the annual sets of six winners could be exchanged for any other, or just as credibly be organized under a different theme entirely. In other words, it is not as if the sound of 2008 is so different from that of 2012 or 2004. So, while there is diversity within a year, there is general homogeneity across the years, with the same differences emerging over time. My own preference would be, conversely, to have homogeneity (or focus) within years and difference between the years. *Never Mind the Bollocks* will always sound like 1977, but at the same time, paradoxically, still sounds fresh. In contrast, the last thirty years of what passes for popular music, let's say the melismatic miasma that swells from Whitney Houston and Celine Dion to the latest contender on *Star Search* or *The Voice,* has no temporal signature and is perpetually stale. It's the choice between intensive significance (how many anthems can you generate from one chord?) and dismissible virtuosity (how many notes can you squeeze into a single syllable?). And signature work requires, or is at least assisted by, a signature jury, one capable of making a statement, of setting a sound for the moment. This is the juror as coconspirator and collaborator, not as talent scout: more Malcolm McLaren than Howie Mandel.

At its most general, thematization represents the end of discipline, and in particular "no precedent" is just another way to say "no discipline." But contrary to the presumed wishes of the theme-makers, the elimination of precedent does not usher in an era of novelty and change: rather, it keeps design captive to the contingencies of the current status quo. Themes are a way to substitute urgencies for urges, earnestness for erotics. Architecture as a discursive field requires the ability to wrangle with what came before, to set out likes and dislikes, form and reform teams and genealogies, invent one's predecessors and rescript the past along with the future. Yet, in all quarters today, thinking through precedents has become a lost attribute, and this is not simply a generational deficit. In place of precedent and break what has emerged is a faith in the perpetual interface of testing. And exactly to the degree that precedent enables worlds of *argumentation,* testing accommodates a practice of *optimization.* Whether under the theme of digital-parametric or sustainable-green, the value of optimization today can only reinforce a naturalist design politics. In this situation, precedent and its deviation are important cultural forms to elude the new masters of fact, the fatalists of self-organization, and promote a synthetic design politics. Fortunately, and despite the theme that would underwrite it, the most interesting work in the pages that follow deploys a self-conscious attitude to fabricating genealogies and debate as a way to inject strangeness into the world. Or better, without resort to the fundamentalisms of either identity or difference, they similarly take on the disciplinary ambition of projecting new worlds. As with the best work today, they concern themselves with engineering values, not value engineering. Like them or leave them, the choice of entertaining these worlds is yours, with the understanding that such choice itself is only possible through the untimeliness offered by precedent.

Introduction
Anne Rieselbach, Program Director
The Architectural League of New York

This year's competition theme, No Precedent, captures the energetic restlessness of a generation of young architects. Driven by the desire to create, they are, in the words of the League Prize Committee, unwilling to wait their turn or to follow in footsteps. The call for entries outlined how young architects and designers are casting aside "unfit precedents" for projects, problems, methodologies, and even spaces of intervention, to create work that is "suggestive, speculative, and on the brink." No Precedent encouraged this strategy, asking for "ideas, works, and methodologies that are unfounded, ungrounded, and suspect…the things no one has done before, and that one has little experience with."

The competition winners addressed both the tension and opportunities inherent in moving beyond comfortable, tried-and-true architectural precedents, whether formal, philosophical, technical, or professional. The work in their portfolios revealed new design strategies, modes of production, and models of practice. Each of them revisited design problems and tested fabrication methods to innovate unprecedented solutions—and all of them extended and expressed this questioning, exploratory way of working in the site-specific installations they created for the League Prize exhibition.

Jimenez Lai is a self-described "architect who tells stories through drawing… to conflate his many curiosities about theory, criticism, design, and representation." He defined his installation, Little Monster, as "super furniture—not big enough to be a building, but too large to be just furniture." Part shelving, part loveseat, with an overscaled presence in elevation, the piece created a framework to house cartoon caption–like cases created by irregularly shaped inner cavities. The surfaces were lined with a variety of materials and textures, from gilded and brightly colored vinyl to patterned fabric, Astroturf, and pink shag carpeting, creating a different environment in each cavity. The piece transformed the stylized narrative structure of Lai's drawings into built form, celebrating "the pluralistic multiplicity that a cartoon page offers—like a big comic book page one can walk into."

An irregular crystalline terrain formed by an interlocking group of faceted oriented strand board pedestals, sutured with plastic zip ties, housed a collection of models, prototypes, and digital media sampling a number of SOFTlab's recent projects, many of them temporary installations utilizing repetitive assembly as a key design component. Capped with one-way mirrored acrylic that changes in opacity and reflectivity based on the viewer's position and the ambient lighting inside the gallery, the faceted pedestals' visually shifting appearance and varied contents were intended to suggest principal Michael Szivos's design approach that is "part of a larger landscape of future strategies, combinations, and possibilities." The dynamic composition typifies SOFTlab's emphasis on finding ways to explore the experiential potential of built projects that physically "engage people and test the limits of what is possible."

MMX's intricately folded wall, suspended across one corner of the gallery, exemplified the integrative strategies of design, structure, and fabrication that shape how the firm defines the program and refines the form of each project. For this installation, to address the need for an easily transported and quickly deployed structure, firm principals Jorge Arvizu, Ignacio del Rio, Emmanuel Ramirez, and Diego Ricalde designed a lightweight, compressible surface that could be shipped from their Mexico City office packed in three compact carry-on-sized boxes. Like many of the firm's realized projects that employ iterative compositions of everyday materials, such as rope or credit cards, to create structure and shape space (illustrated in a take-away brochure with its own folding instructions), MMX's large, draped cardboard wall relied on repetitive origami folding techniques to define the structure and surface of a room within a room.

Bisecting the gallery, the long, slender wood tabletop that displayed stpmj's recent work rested on a piano-hinged base that could fold, along with the hinged tabletop leaves, into uniformly sized portable "briefcases." The modular components are reconfigurable, with bases that can align to the undersides of the leaves by notching into different configurations of CNC-routed grooves. Applying the firm's concern with redefining design "constraints," their accordion-like table addresses the precedent of traditional fixed gallery furniture and adapts it to provide mobility, lightness, and functional flexibility. The narrow tabletop allowed easy visual access to the firm's projects, encouraging multiple vantage points and perspectives. The diagrams, drawings, and models were presented as pages in a book, prompting the visitor to sequentially read the narrative of stpmj's body of work.

Two bands of graphics illustrated the climatically oriented design approach that shapes architectural strategies for Sean Lally's firm, WEATHERS. The firm's name and design focus references atmospheric variables that are the primary determinants for defining a project's architectural program and generating its built form. A lower band

of images was punctuated by concept panels independent of particular designs, but emblematic of the larger initiatives underlying the work. Illustrations of topically related projects above and adjacent to the concept panels pinwheeled from concept headings related to energy, materials, and gradient properties of material energies to their shapes and organizational implications. Visitors read the work as a narrative tracing the shift away from design based on line and surface, to using gradients as a tool to create physical boundaries delineating programs and new formal approaches to design.

Echoing the modular system that conceptually drives their designs, Koji Tsutsui & Associates' installation surveyed recent projects through a series of panels featuring renderings, diagrammatic sketches, and photographs of built work. The projects and accompanying texts examined the firm's wide-ranging design strategies—from hyperlocal concerns of culture, materiality, and place, to an overarching diagrammatic organizational system that provides an open-ended design intended to foster evolution and expansion. Stylized monochromatic models distilled the structures, revealing the massing of individual elements that generate larger configurations of aggregated forms, evidencing a design approach that links a social structure of individuals, family, and community to a formal structure of cells and fractal frameworks. Tsutsui's goal is to create an "architectural order that allows a building to grow and adapt to bring together and re-build communities."

The League Prize Committee sought young practices that expressed "a willingness to work, to test again and again…to negotiate, and work through problems." The League Prize winners' installations, like their winning portfolios, demonstrated their capacity to question the status quo by actively testing the traditional boundaries of architectural design and practice; rewriting design programs; reexamining the topology and nature of site; testing new materials and structures; and, ultimately, creating compelling work that sets new, decidedly open-ended precedents for future exploration.

Biographies

Bureau Spectacular is a Chicago-based operation of architectural affairs led by founder **Jimenez Lai** since 2008. The studio imagines other worlds and engages the design of architecture through storytelling, whether those are beautiful stories about character development, relationships, curiosities, and attitudes; or absurd stories about fake realities that invite enticing possibilities. The stories conflate design, representation, theory, criticism, history, and taste into cartoon pages. These cartoon narratives swerve into the physical world through architectural installations, models, and small buildings. Lai received his MArch from the University of Toronto and is currently an assistant professor at the University of Illinois at Chicago. Before founding his own firm, Lai worked for MOS, AVL, REX, and OMA/Rem Koolhaas in Toronto, Rotterdam, and New York. Lai's first manifesto, *Citizens of No Place* (2012), was published by Princeton Architectural Press; his installation, White Elephant, has been acquired as part of the permanent collection of the Museum of Modern Art in New York.

Koji Tsutsui & Associates is a Tokyo- and San Francisco–based office founded in 2004 by **Koji Tsutsui**. The office has designed numerous projects around the world while observing global economic and architectural developments. Their work adapts the concepts of ancient village organization into designs for modern, environmentally sustainable communities that take advantage of unique site characteristics. These designs are evident not only in the final form of each building, but also in new architectural orders that allow the buildings to adapt to pressures of ongoing growth and changing environment. Tsutsui received his BArch from the University of Tokyo and his MArch from the Bartlett School of Architecture, University College London. He worked under Tadao Ando on projects such as relief housing for victims of the Great Hanshin earthquake, as well as museums and schools, before establishing his own firm. He is the winner of numerous other prizes, including *Architectural Record*'s Design Vanguard 2011.

Established in 2009, **MMX Studio** is a collaborative team based in Mexico City focused on the design process at the various scales of the territory. Founded by **Jorge Arvizu**, **Emmanuel Ramirez**, **Diego Ricalde**, and **Ignacio del Rio**, the quartet's practice is backed by experience in both nationally and internationally renowned architecture studios. Their collaborative design process directly informs their efforts to promote a participatory built environment. Open to any scale of intervention, MMX Studio develops ideas that range from design and installations to architecture and urbanism. Due to its physical, economic, and social context, the team approaches each project as a unique challenge that requires a precise and customized design process for successful conceptualization and completion. Arvizu holds a master's in Construction Management from the Iberoamerican University in Mexico City. Del Rio graduated with a BArch from the National Autonomous University of Mexico (UNAM). Ramirez also has a BArch from UNAM and holds a MArch in Urban Design from the Bartlett School of Architecture, University College London. Ricalde graduated with a BArch from UNAM and received his MArch in Architecture and Urbanism from the Architectural Association in London.

SOFTlab is a New York City design studio created by **Michael Szivos**, who received his MArch from Columbia University's Graduate School of Architecture, Planning and Preservation. The studio is involved in the design and production of projects across almost every medium, from digitally fabricated large-scale sculpture to interactive design and immersive digital video installations. SOFTlab's unique blend of backgrounds, including designers, artists, architects, and educators, allows the studio to approach every project from a fresh perspective and create rich spatial, graphic, interactive, and visual experiences. By mixing research, creativity, and technology with a strong desire to make working fun, SOFTlab attempts to create new and unique experiences. In 2010 the studio was selected for the New Practices New York award by the AIA New York Chapter. The studio has also produced a wide range of design projects and collaborated with various artists, designers, publications, and institutions including MoMA, the Metropolitan Museum of Art, the *New York Times, eVolo, Surface,* Columbia University, and Pratt Institute.

stpmj is an idea-driven architecture practice based in Brooklyn, New York, founded in 2009 by principals **Seung Teak Lee** and **Mi Jung Lim**. Their work is informed by careful observations of material, structure, program, and typology, and extends to contemporary phenomena (whether social, cultural, political, environmental, or economic). Lee graduated with a BE / ME from Korea University and received his MArch from Harvard's Graduate School of Design, where he was the recipient of the 2009 Department of Architecture Faculty Design Award and a finalist for the SOM Prize in Architecture, Design, and Urban Design. Lim received her BS from Yonsei University, BArch from the Rhode Island School of Design, and MArch from the Graduate School of Design. Prior to stpmj, Lee trained at nARCHITECTS and LEVENBETTS in New York and Herzog & de Meuron in Basel; Lim trained at Office dA in Boston and Andrew Berman Architect in New York.

WEATHERS was founded in 2005 and is based out of Chicago. Its recent projects include proposals for the Gdansk Museum of World War II, an extension to the Stockholm City Library, and a proposal for the urban redevelopment of Reykjavik, Iceland. Principal **Sean Lally** was a coeditor and contributor to *Softspace* (2007) and guest editor of *Energies: New Material Boundaries* (2009). He is the author of the forthcoming book *The Air on Other Planets: A Brief History of Things to Come*. Lally is the recipient of the 2012 Prince Charitable Trusts Rome Prize from the American Academy in Rome in Landscape Architecture and is currently an assistant professor at the University of Illinois at Chicago.

Bureau Spectacular
Jimenez Lai

Phalanastery Module
Los Angeles, California, 2008

This project rotates 360 degrees once every hour. Every fifteen minutes, a plan becomes a section and, in turn, a section becomes a reflected ceiling plan. The gravity-defiance idea was born out of the story "Noah's Ark in Space," about a mass exodus from Earth to a distant planet.

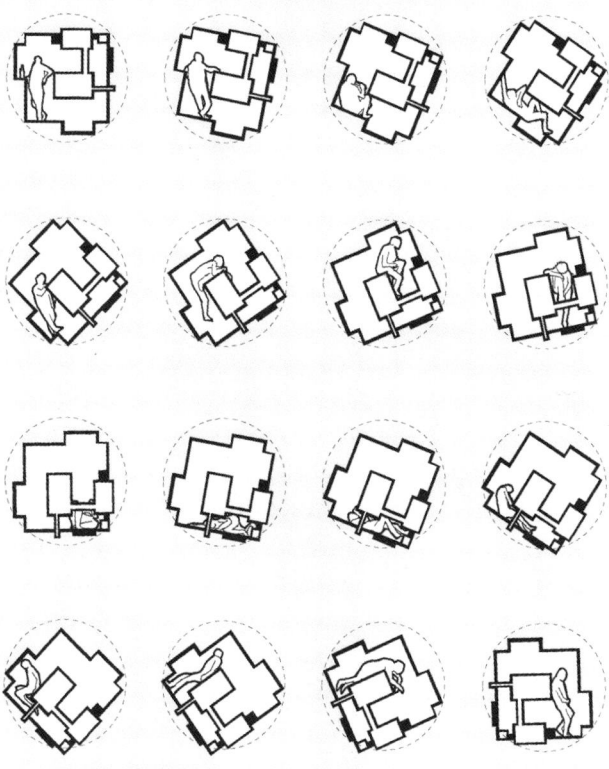

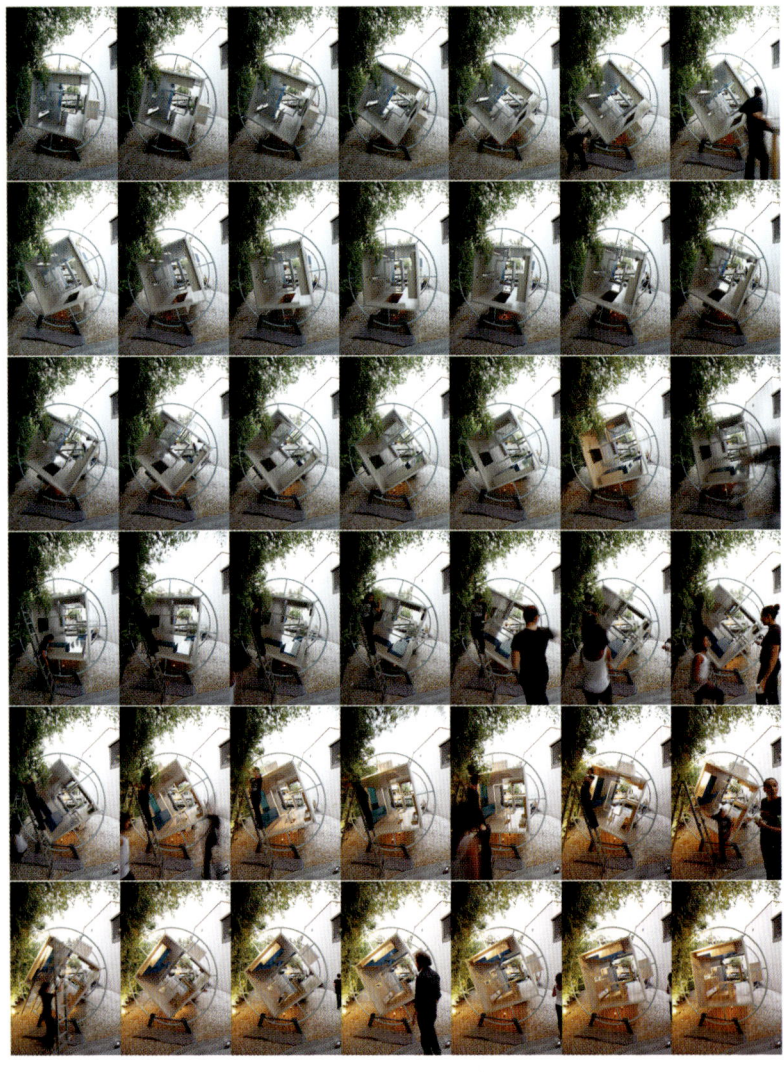

Point Clouds
Chicago, Illinois, 2009

This project is an interactive grid that deforms with pushing and pulling of its points. It uses a set of standard modules to compose a web, and the rotary joints enable the installation to be soft and malleable. The human-sized point cloud engages parametricism.

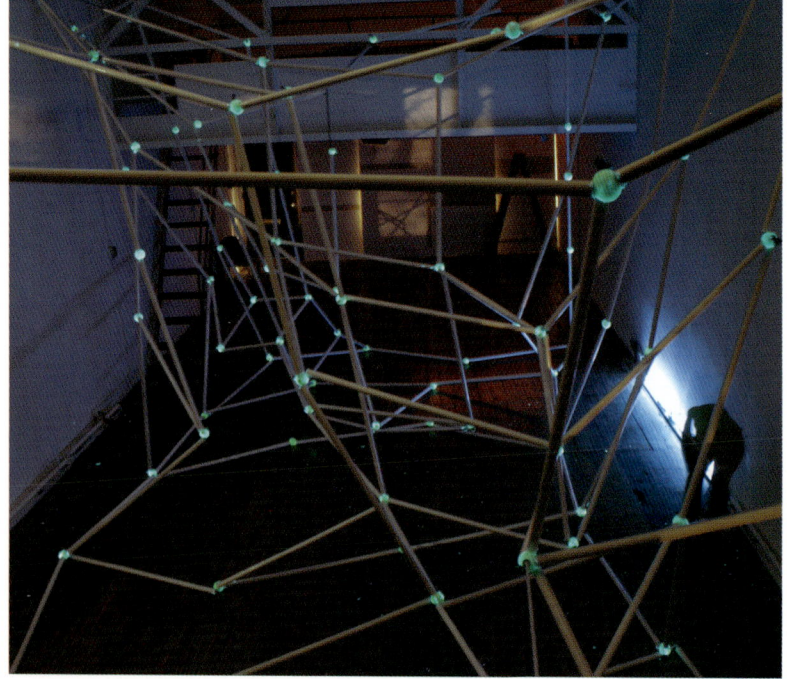

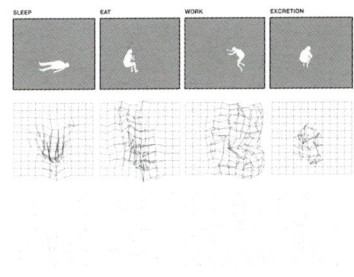

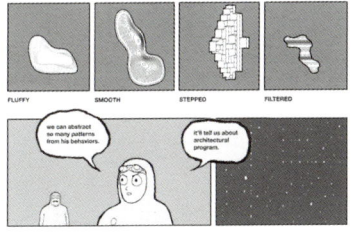

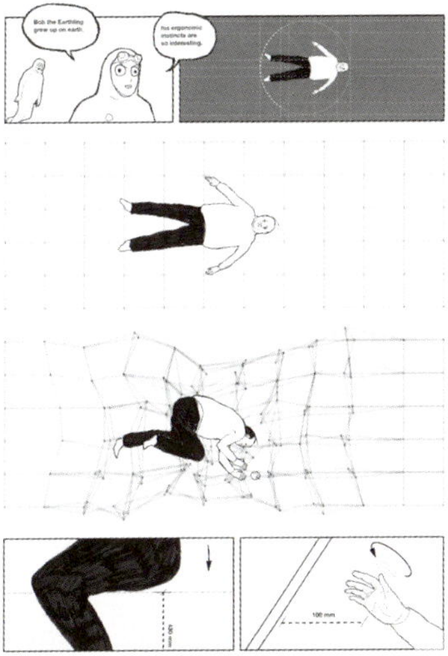

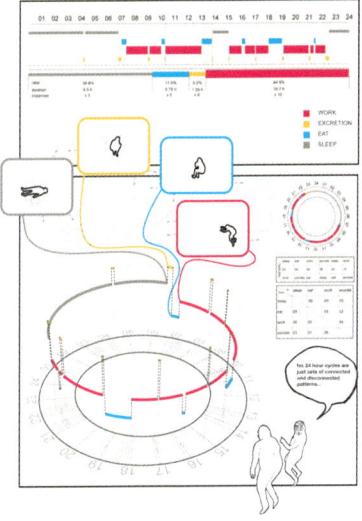

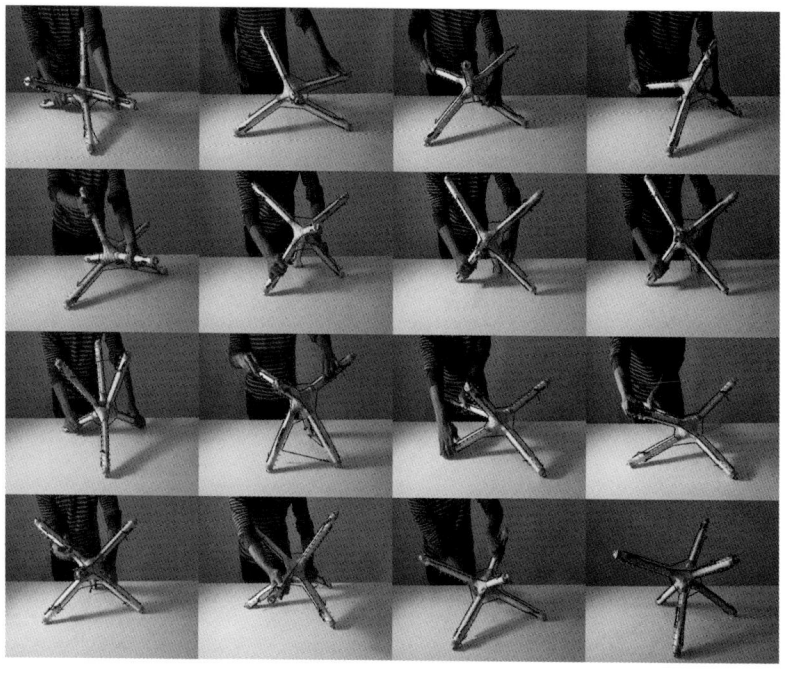

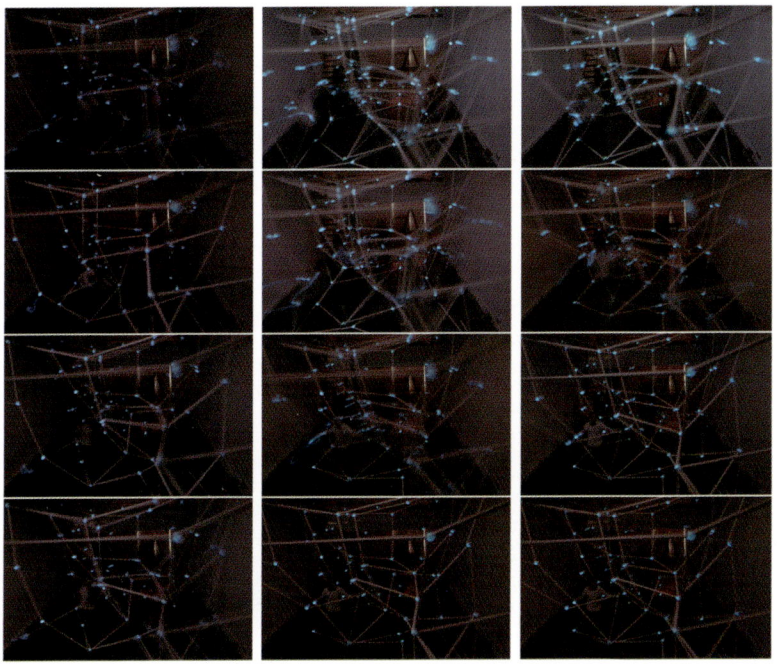

Briefcase House
Chicago, Illinois, 2010

This project is a house inside a house, itself located within an unpartitioned warehouse loft of 1,400 square feet. The design engages two architectural issues: inside / outside and size / scale. The residual gap from the outside of the Briefcase House to the limits of the warehouse loft can be considered a super wall cavity available for programming.

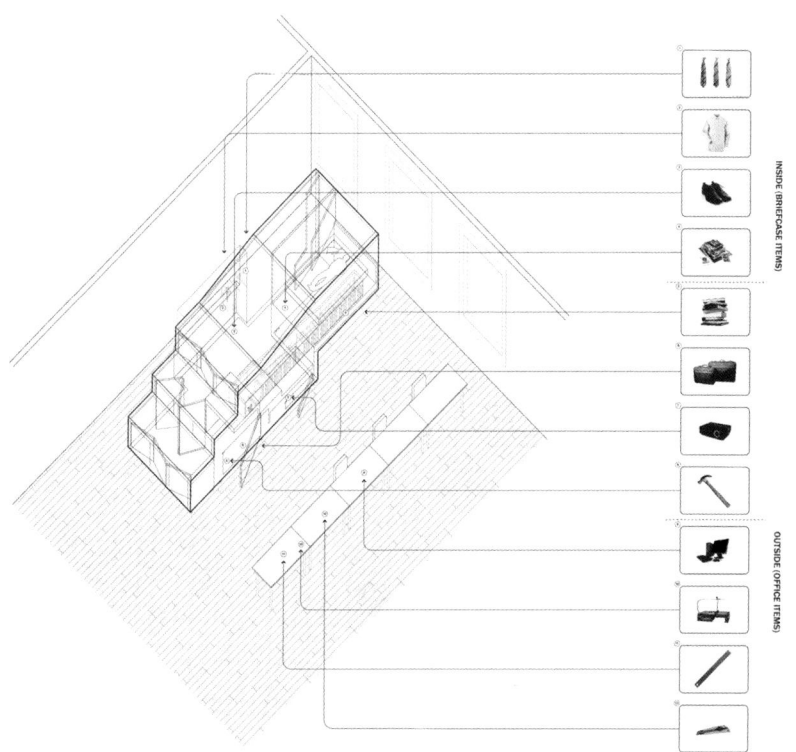

INSIDE (BRIEFCASE ITEMS)

OUTSIDE (OFFICE ITEMS)

THIS PROJECT ENCAPSULATES PERSONAL ITEMS

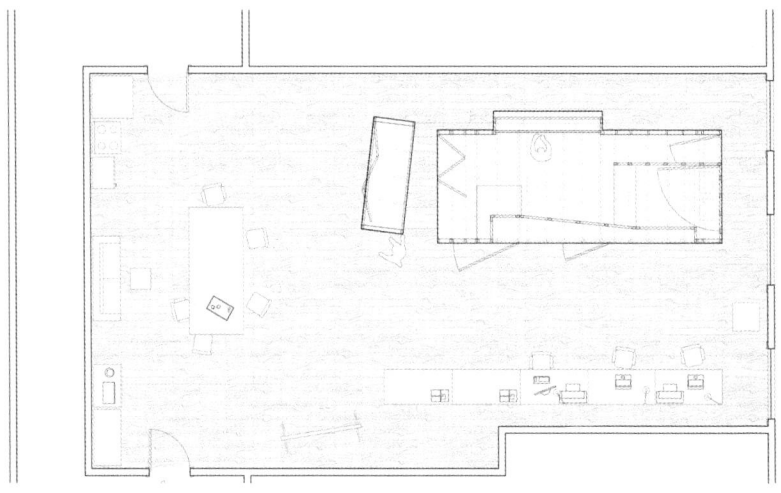

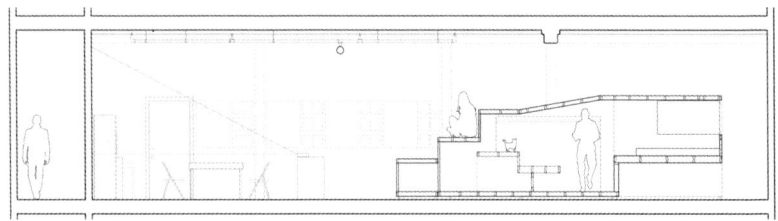

Primitives

2011

This is a story about a primitive hunter who kills a deer but keeps only the hide, which he recomposes into a cloak. He uses the cloak to cover himself, thereby discovering cladding. Dancing under its cover, he can still express his emotions by the rough outlines of his posture. Through this event, the hunter and his lover discover the concept of abstraction.

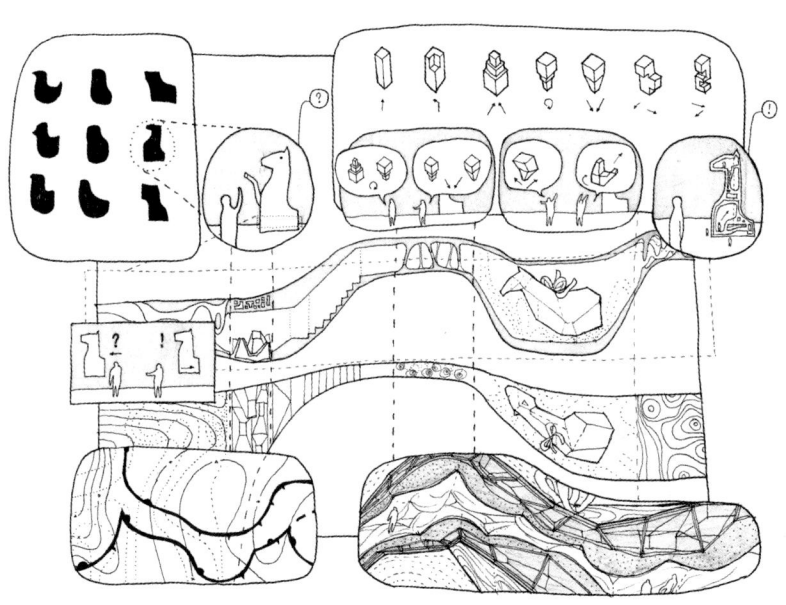

abstraction of outside / fluidity of inside

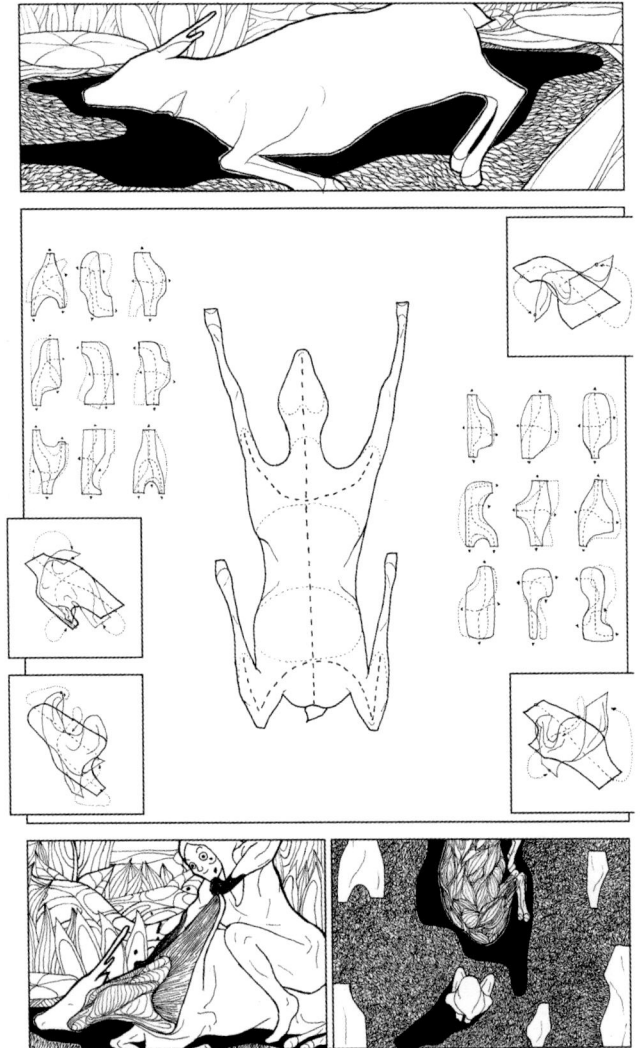

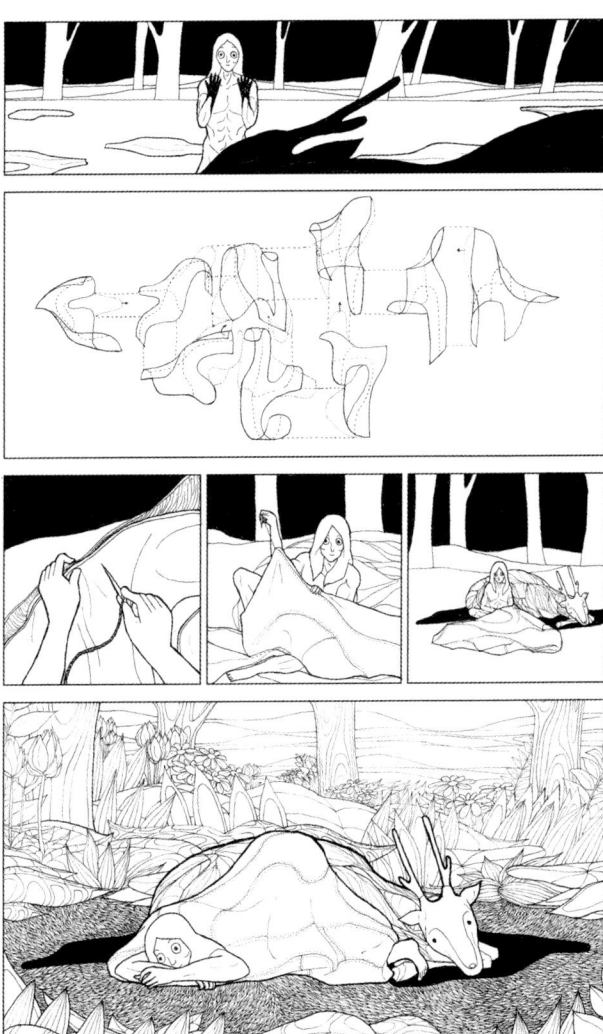

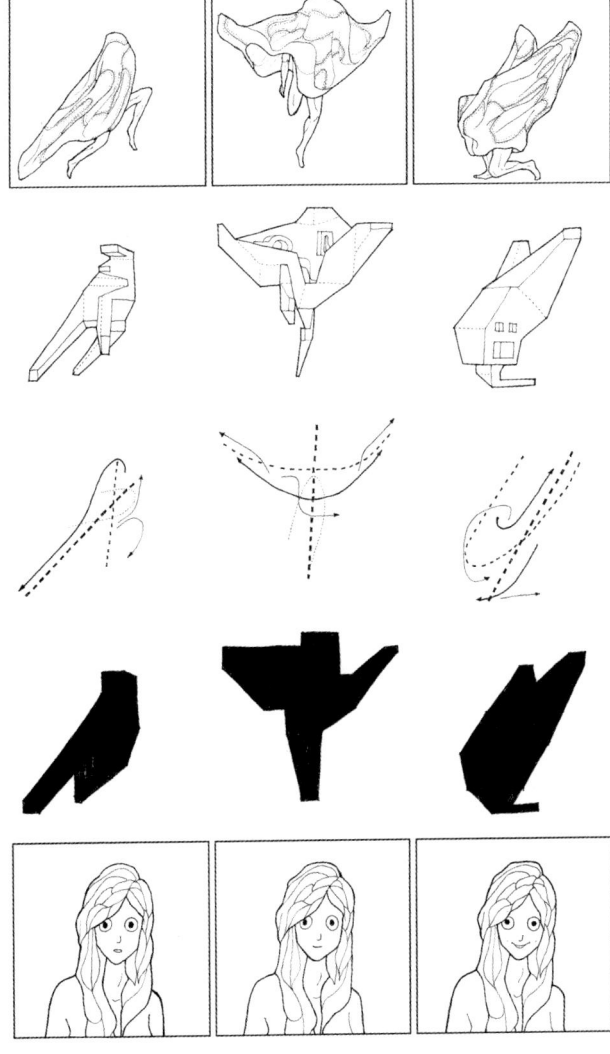

White Elephant (Privately Soft)
Louisville, Kentucky, 2011

This is a building that can tumble freely without fixed orientations. It is hard on the outside but soft on the inside, and it obstructs the continuity of interior spaces like an elephant in a room. This installation is a freestanding micro building and a piece of macro furniture that questions projection, inside/outside, rigidity/fluidity, and size/scale.

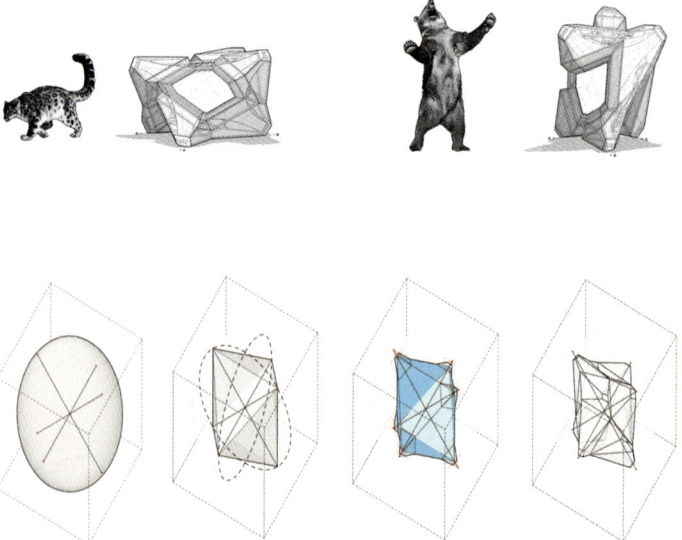

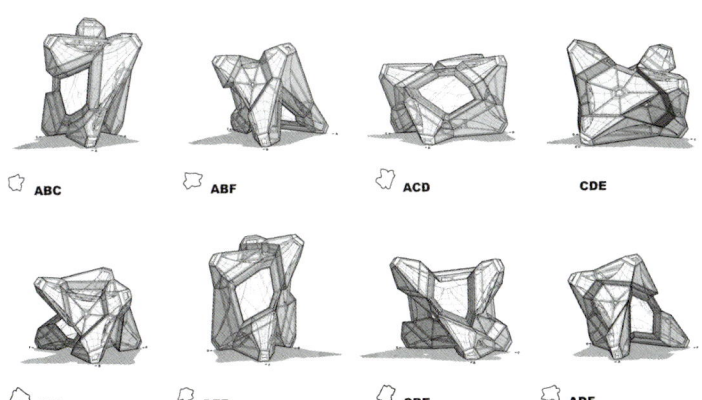

ABC

ABF

ACD

CDE

BEF

DEF

CBE

ADF

Koji Tsutsui & Associates

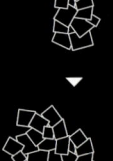

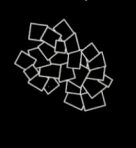

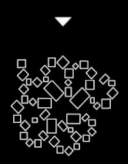

In an unprecedented time, when a financial crisis and catastrophic disasters are so prevalent in the world, families and communities are growing apart in many places. Architects must be involved in these issues and design projects to promote sustainability and build communities.

For the past five years in San Francisco, Koji Tsutsui & Associates have been doing just that, working on designs, for instance, to adapt ancient villages for community building and vernacular architecture for cultural and environmental sustainability. Each of these projects has unique contextual conditions that are resolved in a new architectural order. Our unprecedented approach takes shape in the establishment of a new architectural order that allows a building to grow and adapt to create and develop communities.

A community is a fractal structure where individuals form a family, and families create a community. Similarly, our projects are architectural fractal systems where the rooms cluster around a common space, and buildings cluster around a courtyard like people holding hands in a circle. Rooms (cells), the smallest functional units of a building, are placed on each site at the best orientation for the existing conditions to form a multicellular building with overlapping loop circulations or a village with multiple courtyards where people can interact.

For cultural sustainability, traditional construction techniques are integrated into modern construction technology to keep the culture alive. For environmental sustainability, a building is constructed to allow growth and alterations with time, prolonging building life.

Mill Valley House
Mill Valley, California, 2012

This house sits on a steeply sloped site next to the San Francisco Bay. Designed to minimize the disturbance of the surrounding environment, the prefabricated wood-frame boxes (rooms) are rotated so that spaces interlock with one another to create continuous loop circulation and allow an infinite sequence of spaces. The rooms are elevated on steel pilotis to match the topography, allowing native plants to grow and stabilize the soil, and deer and squirrels to roam underneath. It will start as a single-family dwelling and grow to accommodate multiple families.

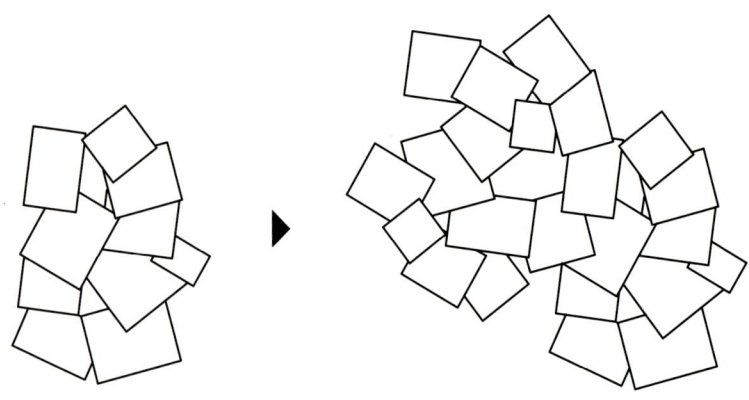

1

2

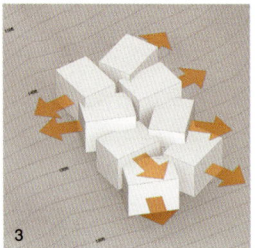

3

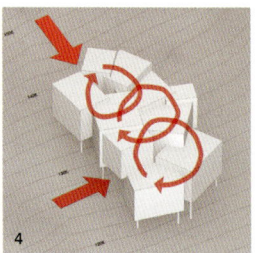

4

1: Plan expansion diagram
2: Mass and floor elevation study
3: View, solar orientation, and circulation study

4: Continuous loop circulations and approach study
5: Main entrance: roof harvesting rain

5

6: Site plan
7: House in the forest*
8: Dining room*

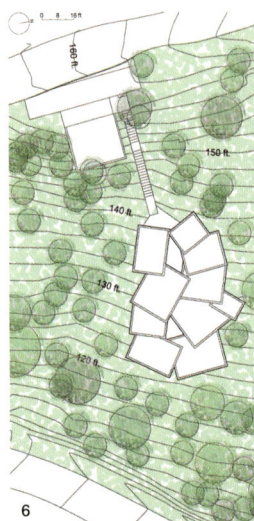

9: House elevated to match topography*
10: Original plan *(one-family dwelling)*

11: Sustainability section diagram
**photo credit: Iwan Baan*

9

10

11

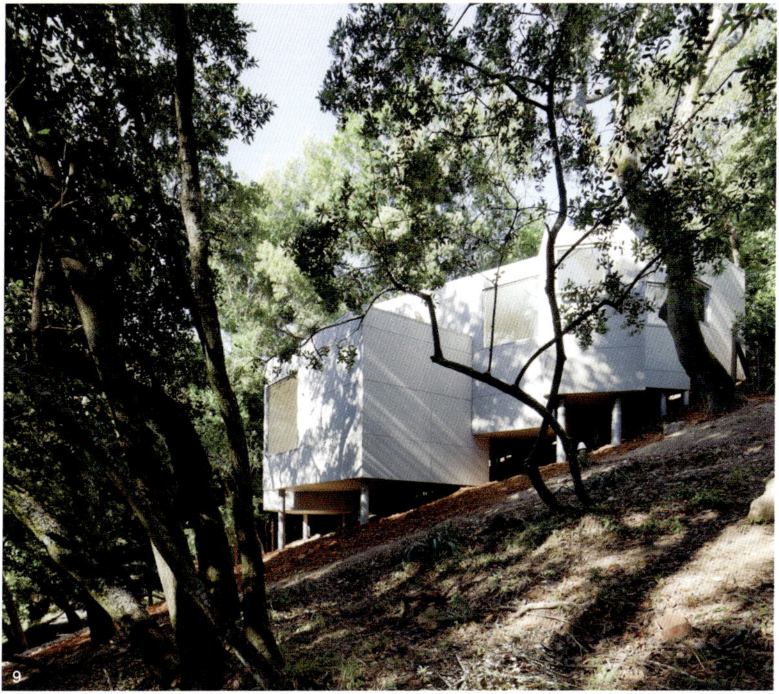

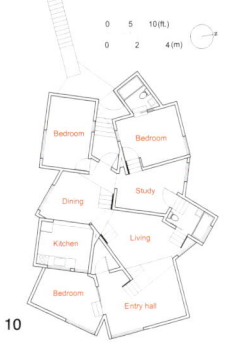

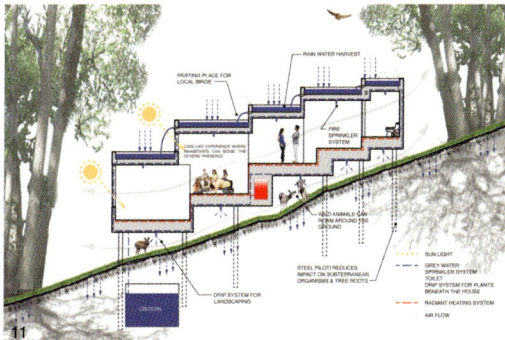

Yutenji House

Tokyo, Japan, 2011

The clients were a couple, two musicians who wanted home-office spaces in the house. We conceived the house as tightly stacked boxes, creating a vertical village where the clients could live and work as a microcommunity. From the program, we determined sizes for each room's function and stacked those to fit within a strict building envelope. Each room can be built with a standard wood-frame construction method. Since the client's father is constructing the house, we designed it so that he will be able to add rooms to the house in the future without compromising the architectural integrity.

1

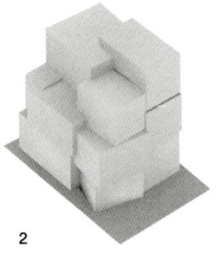

2

3

4

1: Rooms as boxes
2: Stacking boxes to meet architectural
requirements and program

3: Structural framing
4: Final form and roof garden
5: View from street

5

6: Plans
7: View from street

8: Family room
9: Stair runs through the boxes' in-between space

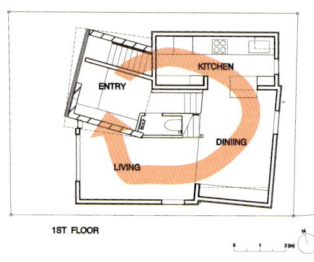

1ST FLOOR

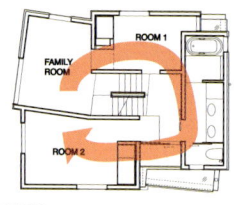

2ND FLOOR

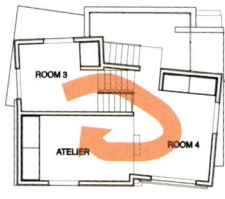

3RD FLOOR

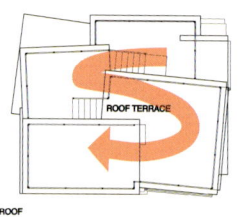

ROOF

6

7

8

9

10: View from the street
11: Wood framing during the construction phase
12: Box layering visible from living room window

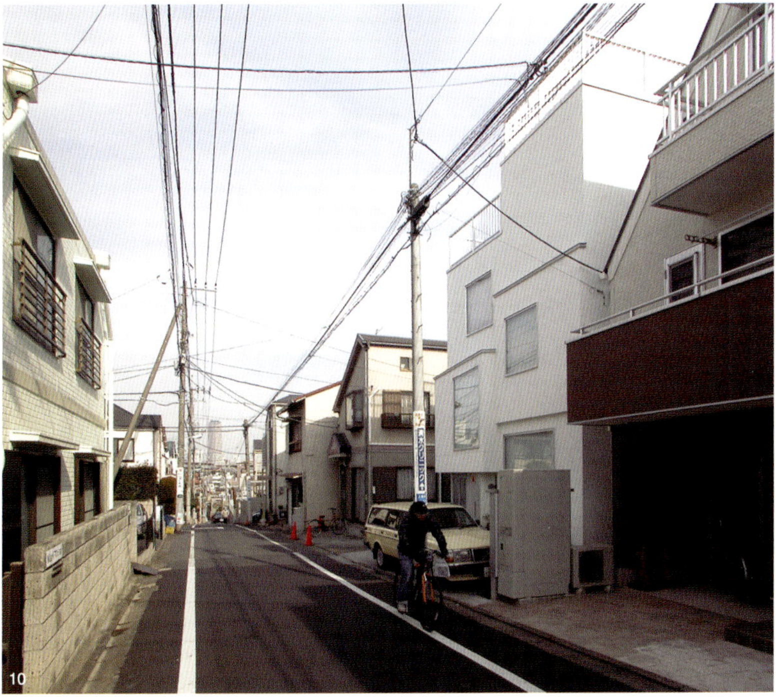

10

11

12

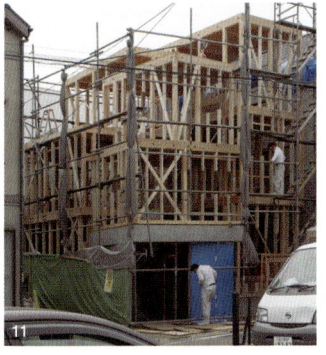

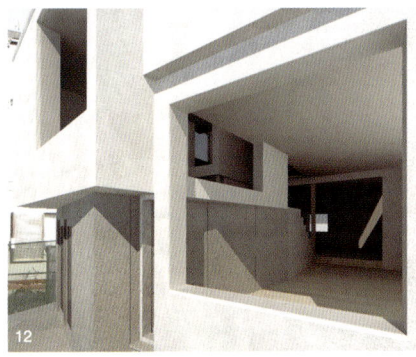

InBetween House
Karuizawa, Japan, 2010

The house consists of five cottages with single-pitched roofs clad in local larch wood siding. It was built in a traditional Japanese wood construction method and local builders skillfully crafted each structural wood member. Triangular roofs between the cottages direct the in-between space into a fluid public interior space, which functions as a living room or circulation space. These in-between spaces are like alleys in a city looking off at the mountains in the distance.

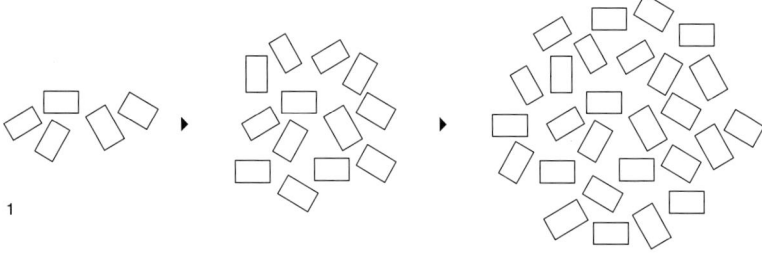

1

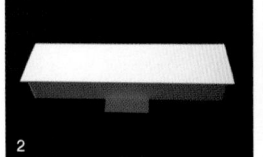

2

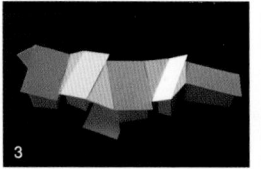

3

4

1: Plan expansion diagram
2: Mass model
3: Linear model
4: Cluster model

5: South elevation from driveway: cottages, folding roof, and thin roof eaves*
6: Main InBetween space: living room*

7: North elevation from surrounding woods*
8: Roof plan
9: Reflecting ceiling plan showing roof structure

10: Plan
11: InBetween space: sunroom*

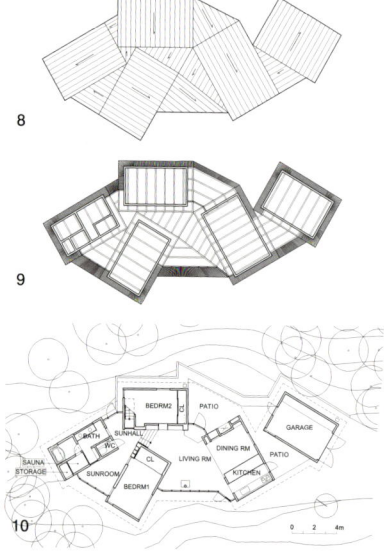

12: West elevation*
13: Entry; gaps between cottages become circulation space.*

**photo credit: Iwan Baan*

12

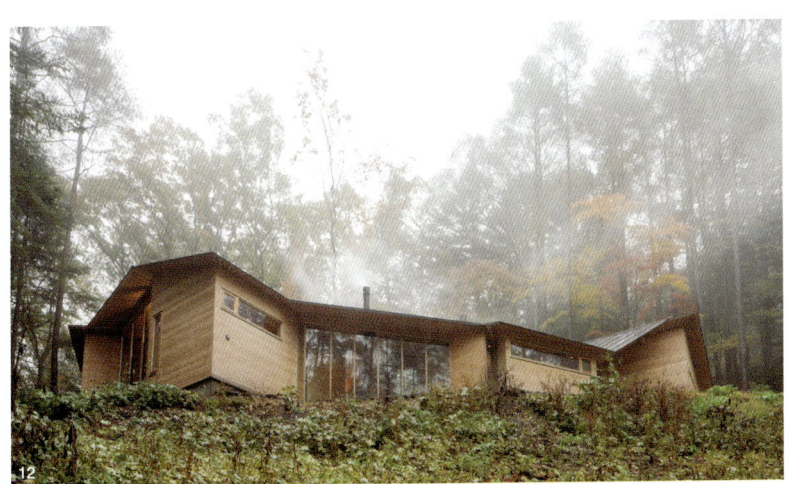

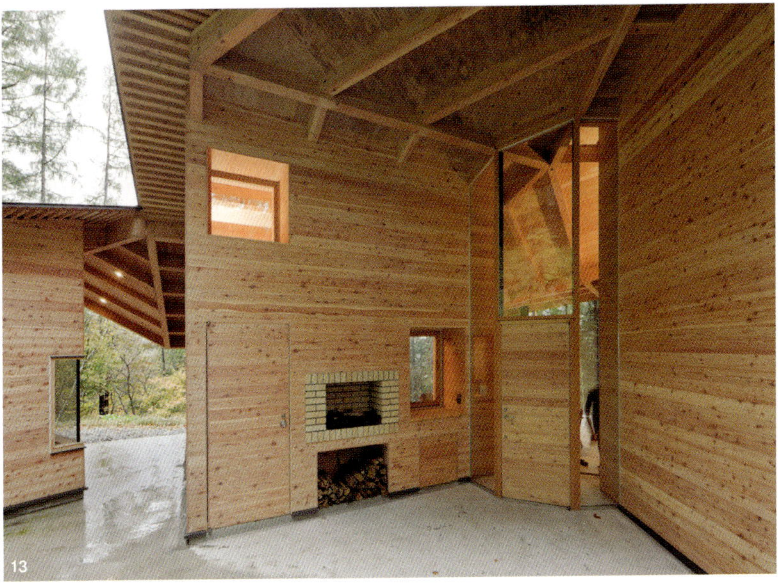
13

Mission in Haiti
Haiti, 2009

In 2009 we were given a volunteer opportunity by a nonprofit organization to design a religious facility in Haiti. We reexamined a project in Uganda (see page 64) and systemized each brick unit and the site plan for time and cost efficiency. It is designed to grow over time with a church at the center of development, and expand with the addition of a school and dormitory for foster mothers and orphans to become a building complex like a traditional monastery. The church space encompasses six units with a lattice roof to let in sunlight.

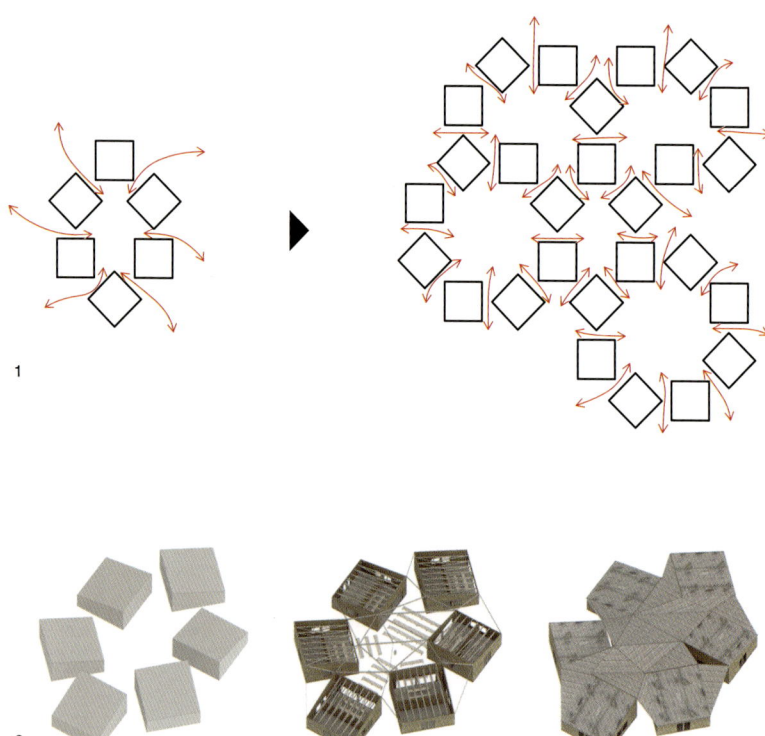

1

2

1: Plan expansion diagram
2: Massing study of church (left), church units and structure (center), and church roof (right)

3: Interior of church
4: Church elevation

5: Plan
6: Bird's-eye view of expanded plan

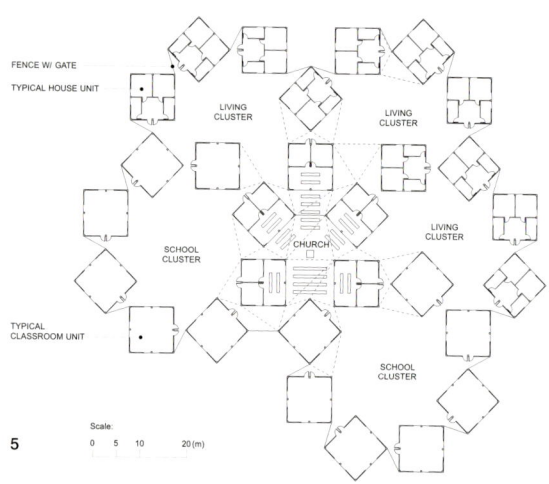

FENCE W/ GATE

TYPICAL HOUSE UNIT

LIVING CLUSTER

LIVING CLUSTER

LIVING CLUSTER

SCHOOL CLUSTER

CHURCH

TYPICAL CLASSROOM UNIT

SCHOOL CLUSTER

5

Scale:
0   5   10   20 (m)

6

7: Bird's-eye view of church
8: Interior of church

School and Home for HIV Orphans
Uganda, 2008

This project houses orphans who have lost their parents to Uganda's HIV/AIDS epidemic. It allows them to live in a familial community and to have the ability to build their own homes using local building methods. The initial eight huts huddle in a cluster with an old tree at the center, around which children hold their studies.
As the children grow, they will use their construction knowledge to add more huts and expand the orphanage into a real village. The original architecture will ultimately become a focal point of the future village.

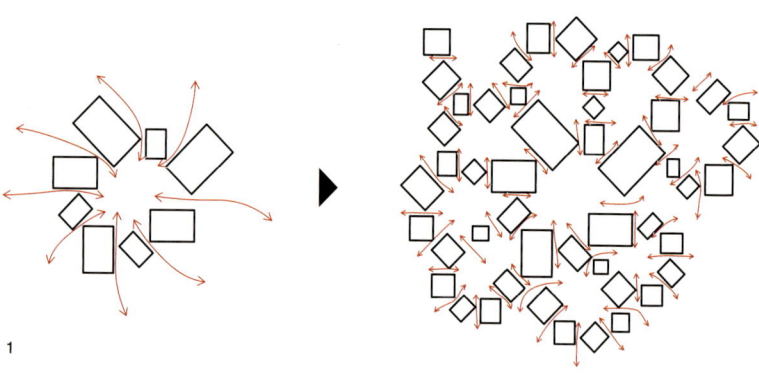

1

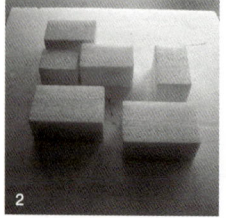

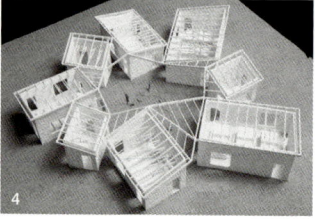

2   3   4

1: Plan expansion diagram
2: Urban model: small courtyard, institutional appearance, grid system, lacks sense of community
3: Cluster model: large courtyard, similar to indigenous villages, radial system, well-defined community
4: Space and structural model

5: Center courtyard; primitive huts connected by canopies huddle around a courtyard, which becomes a children's home.
6: Plan
7: Construction phase; huts surround existing tree in center courtyard.
8: Elevation

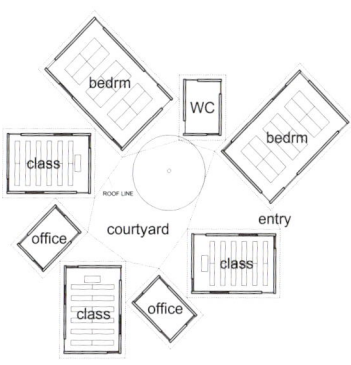

6

8

9: Orphanage expands to become
a village in the future
10: Plan: orphanage becomes a village

11: Elevation sketch
12: Plan

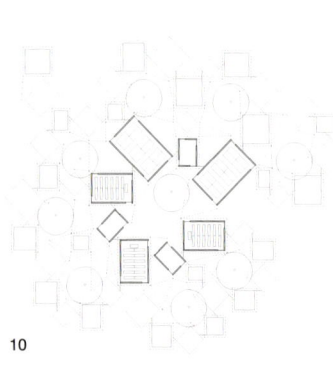

10

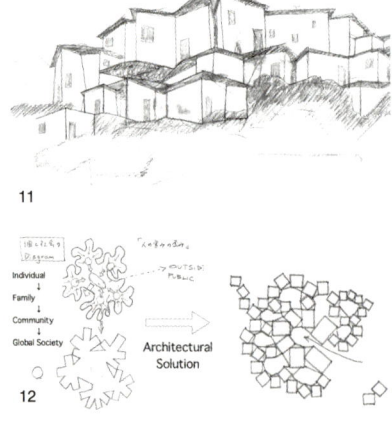

11

12

13: Model photo from above showing the roofscape
14: Model photo from below showing network
of courtyards

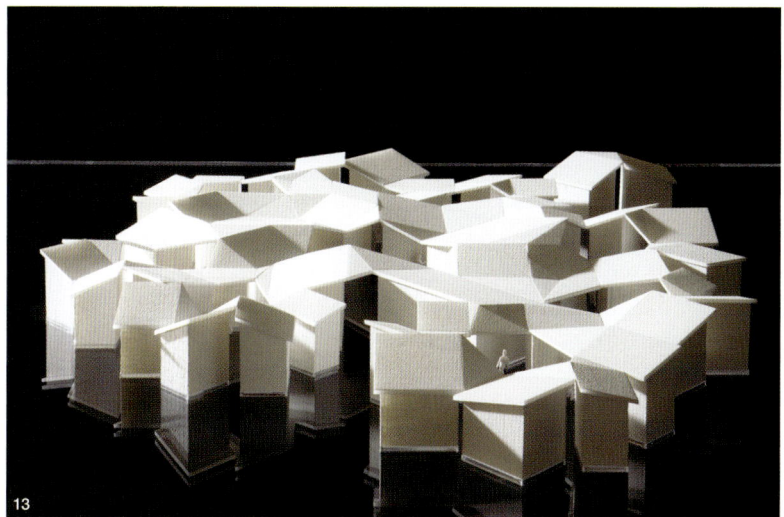

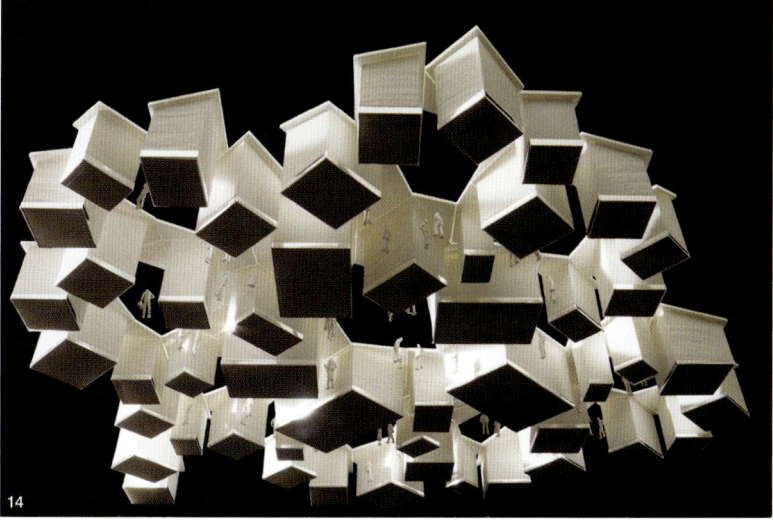

Industrial Designer House
Tokyo, Japan, 2007

This house was designed for an industrial designer with very high expectations. Public and private spaces are separated, while internal openings subtly connect all spaces to make the division between working and living space ambiguous. All the elements of the house form a primitive space consisting of architectural components such as floor, wall, ceiling, stairs, void, and openings. The result is internal space as abstract substance: a valley of walls on the third floor, for instance, or a refreshing expanse in the living/dining room on the second floor, or a cave-like study and garage on the ground floor; everything is woven together into a landscape that offers a variety of sceneries for living and designing.

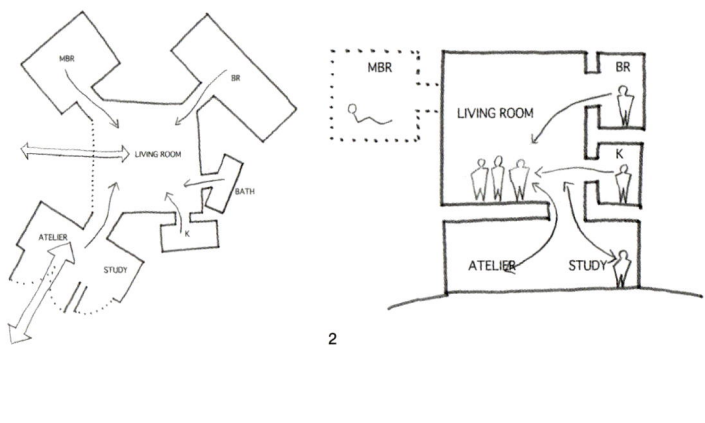

1

2

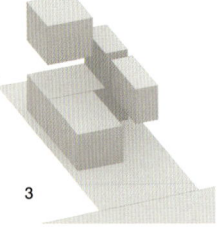

3

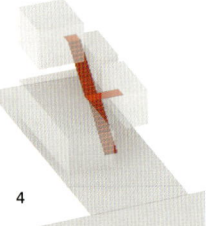

4

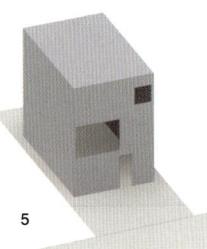

5

1–2: Plan and section concepts
3: Stacked rooms
4: Circulation
5: Skin

6: Living / dining room; interior openings
subtly connect adjacent spaces.*
7: South elevation: steel exterior cladding*
8: Balcony looking down into the living / dining room*

9: Night view: open to the outside*

10: Living / dining room
11: Cave-like garage looking into the study*

12: Stair running between room masses*
photo credit: Masao Nishikawa

10

11

12

MMX Studio

Jorge Arvizu / Emmanuel Ramirez / Diego Ricalde / Ignacio del Rio

After winning the League Prize, we wanted to revisit our work. We discovered that precedents are everywhere. Whatever we read, see, or think we know can be traced to ideas that themselves once seemed unprecedented. But if that's the case, we wondered—if we acknowledge that there is no way to escape this baggage—how can we create something with no precedent? How can we separate our ideas from previous work?

The formal results of our work bring coherence to a variety of different pieces. Seen from a broader perspective, this articulation of components is larger than the intervention itself. Our design is not arbitrarily determined; on the contrary, it emerges from the thoughtful study of our environment and everyday experience. Observing details that we might otherwise ignore helps an unprecedented idea to emerge.

Our design strategy deliberately moves us away from traditional formal creation. For instance, we look to the context of our interventions to directly inform their design. The relation between the environment and both the intervention and its content is the driving force that informs our ideas and the outcome of our work. These structures, once implemented, then redefine the properties of the original environment. This ability to understand and rearticulate existing logics into completely new typologies allows us to produce unprecedented ideas.

Our goal is not the intervention itself, but the synergy triggered by its components. This approach focuses our attention on the process of generating public and private space, the definition of interior and exterior, and the ambiguities in between, yielding different degrees of interaction between the interventions and their environment.

No Precedent Installation

Parsons The New School for Design, New York, New York, 2009

Modifying the gallery context, the intervention engages the space through an interface that creates an anonymous backdrop in relation to the rest of the exhibition. The result is a room within a room, where visitors can calmly sit and reflect upon the context, the new container, and its contents in a tranquil environment.

Transportation and fabrication proved to be the fundamental challenges of the design process. The vast surface of the structure had to be transported internationally in carry-on luggage. We used the ancient Japanese art of origami as inspiration. The origami technique offered the performative characteristics needed to answer the challenge and became the model for our installation solution, creating a collapsible prefabricated system that allowed easy transport and efficient assembly. It allowed us to transport a design of unprecedented scale range, whose volume expanded from hand luggage to the space of architecture.

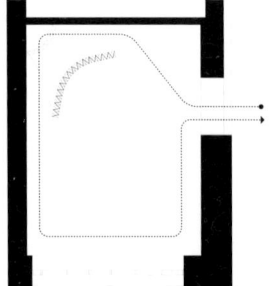

1

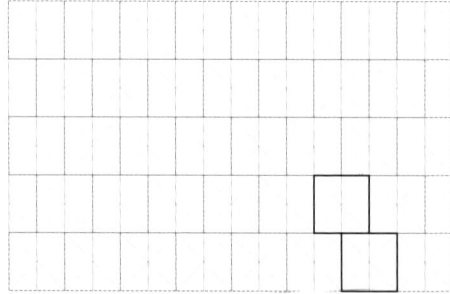

2

1: Floor plan of the gallery
2: Origami pattern
3: Interior view

4: Interior view
5: Detail of the internal pattern

6: Front view
7: Folding pattern

8: Detail of the external pattern
9: Packing

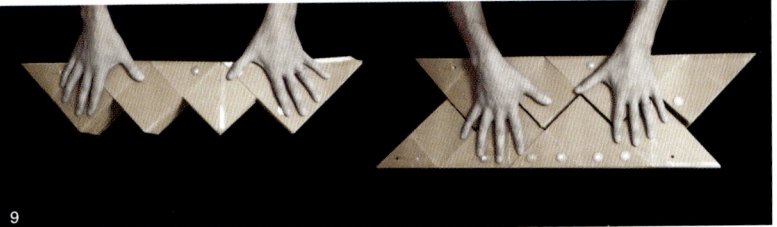

8

9

Fashion's Night Out Pavilion
Luis Adelantado Gallery, Mexico City, Mexico, 2011

As part of the global one-day celebration dedicated to fashion, Fashion's Night Out asked various artists to contribute to an event held at a renowned gallery in Mexico City. Special materials and space were assigned to each artist to transform into pieces that would be donated to a nonprofit.

MMX Studio was assigned the entrance hall of the gallery to work with. Deciding to avoid the obvious route, we created an installation that fully involved the actual space itself. Our strategy strengthened the museography and reinforced movement by creating a screen that allowed visitors to see the entire gallery at once and follow a natural flow past the register as they entered the heart of the exhibition.

Working within the existing confined space instead of trying to define it is an exercise that architects seldom attempt. This installation benefited from the redefinition of such limits and explored the experiential impact that scale, character, and repetition can have upon an object in space. As a result, the object and the space merge together in such a way that a new configuration of the original space naturally emerges.

Textiles and patterns are fundamental to fashion, so we decided to use our special material, an unlimited number of deactivated credit cards, to create an additive system that could generate a tridimensional textile to transform the entrance hall. More than 16,000 cards were assembled and the resulting canvas worked just like textiles; a simple fold could restructure the special properties of the site with minimal effort.

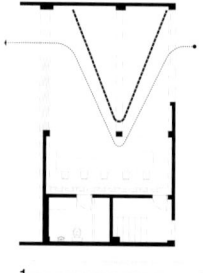

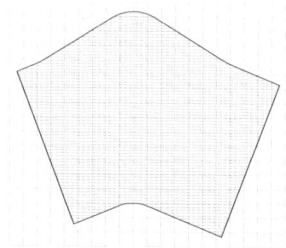

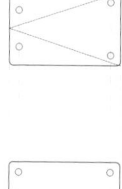

1   2   3

1: Floor plan, gallery reception
2: Unfolded geometry of the textile

3: Card types
4: Interior view

4

5: Detail
6–7: Views from the gallery hall

8: Assembly

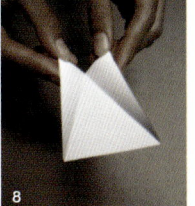   

ECO Pavilion

El Eco Experimental Museum, Mexico City, Mexico, 2010

In 2011 MMX Studio entered and won a competition organized by El Eco Experimental Museum in Mexico City for a temporary event space on the main patio of the building. The winning design does not seek to create a stand-alone piece in the courtyard; on the contrary, the intervention tries to strengthen the key assets of the original museum, creating an extension of the architectural experiment that the original building pursues.

The midcentury building, designed by artist Mathias Goeritz, is an interwoven sequence of emotions crafted with a carefully envisioned progression of crooked spaces and changing light intensity. Our design acknowledges Goeritz's intentions with a pavilion that creates a new chain of perceptual events linked to the original sequence. The intervention is a field operation that encourages the visitor to move around the space to discover new fields, sights, and perspectives. The design is a nonstructural extension of the original museum, an icon of twentieth-century Mexican architecture.

The pavilion, composed primarily of rope and shadow, features two interwoven systems of lines running freely through the museum's two courtyards. The newly created three-dimensional surfaces form screens of varying densities that reconfigure the openness of the original spaces into smaller enclosures. On the museum's main patio the pavilion becomes a series of rope systems, a repeating geometric ceiling that completely alters the space and experience. The angular sloping structure also fills the courtyard with shadows, which constantly change with the sun's path.

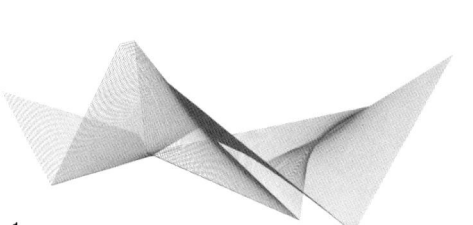

1

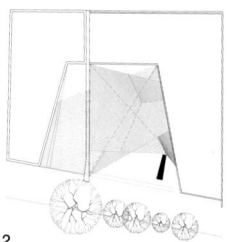

2

1: Overall configuration of the rope systems
2: Roof plan
3: View from the main courtyard

3

4–6: Views from the main courtyard

7: View from the window toward the courtyard
8: Detail

CSC House

Santa Catarina, Morelos, Mexico, 2011

Primarily organized around an existing tree, the framework for CSC House is structured and subdivided to respond to the site's context. The proposal's volumes and open space revolve around the tree's central position, creating a new field-based framework that gives both hierarchy and structure to the design across its different scales.

The site's subdivision reflects a strategy of two- and three-dimensional fragmentation, responding to the site's existing topography. As it adapts to local conditions, the scheme creates a repeating sequence of similar elements and spaces that complement one another. This creates a group of three residential units shaped by interactions between the object, the site, and the surrounding landscape. The volumes are programmed and positioned along the central patio and feature striking views of the surrounding landscape. The resulting geometry is the result of relationships between programmed spaces and their hierarchy. In reinterpreting a traditional pitched-roof house, the design yields a pair of interlocked volumes shaped by internal forces of program within parameters defined by the immediate context.

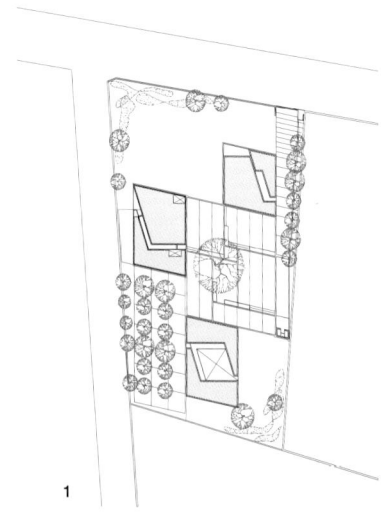

1

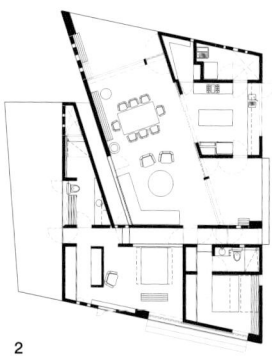

2

1: Site plan
2: Floor plan house 1
3: External view

4–5: Interior views
6: External view

7: External view
8–10: Wall details

7

8

9

10

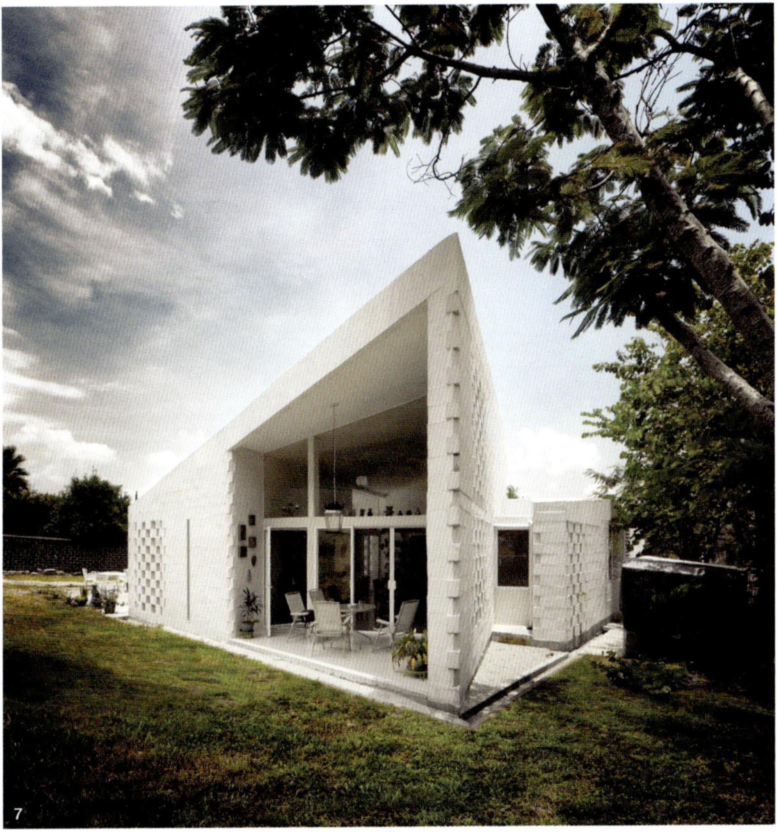

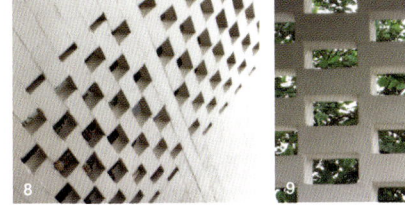

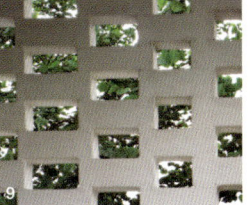

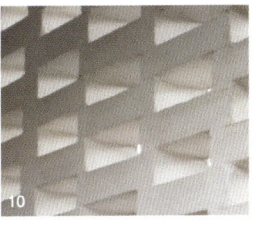

Cancun Cathedral

Cancun, Mexico, 2009

Designing a cathedral presented us with the opportunity to create a landmark that reinforced a population's historically strong Christian faith. It also forced us to reflect upon the constant dialogue that should take place in a territory full of culture and history.

Light and stone symbolize the way volumes and spaces explore dual interactions at various scales, conveyed through solidness/emptiness and open space or built form. Furthermore, the distribution of the program's exterior and interior spaces is laid out as a reinterpretation of traditional religious compounds, keeping a clear and precise relationship between each other.

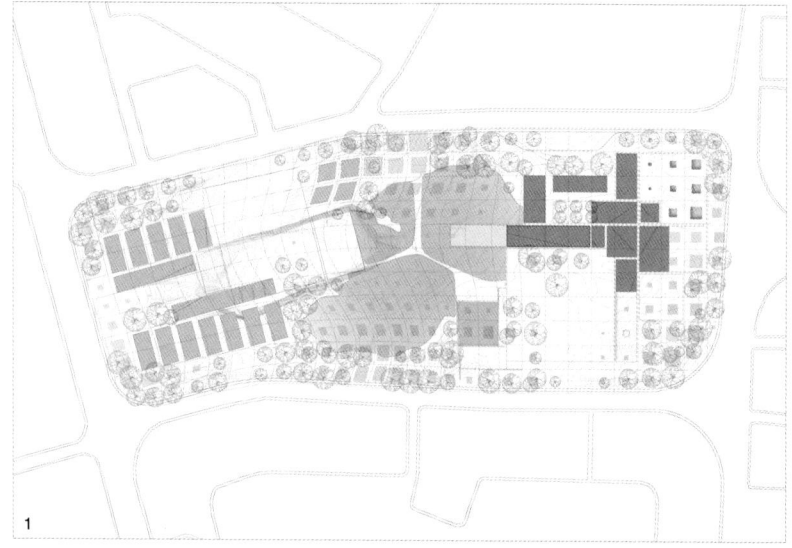

1

1: Site plan
2: View from the entrance square

2

3: Interior view
4: Floor plan
5: Section

3

4

5

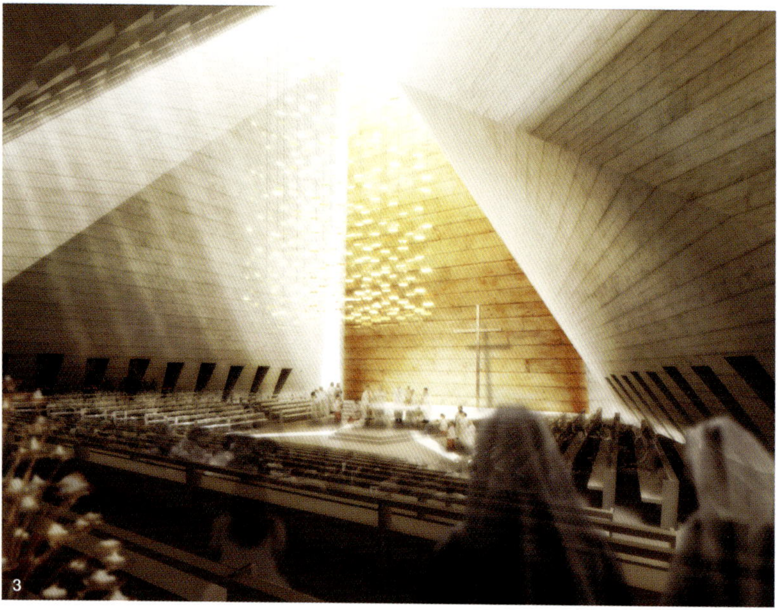

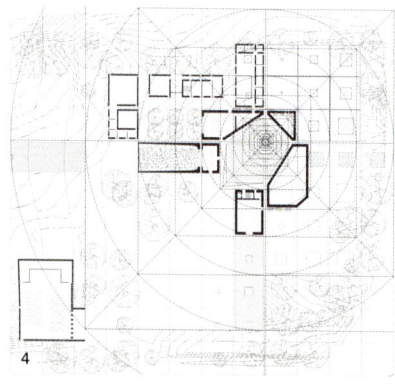

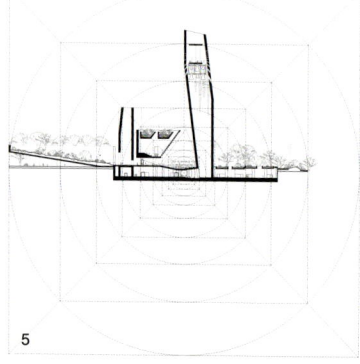

6: Interior view
7: Study model

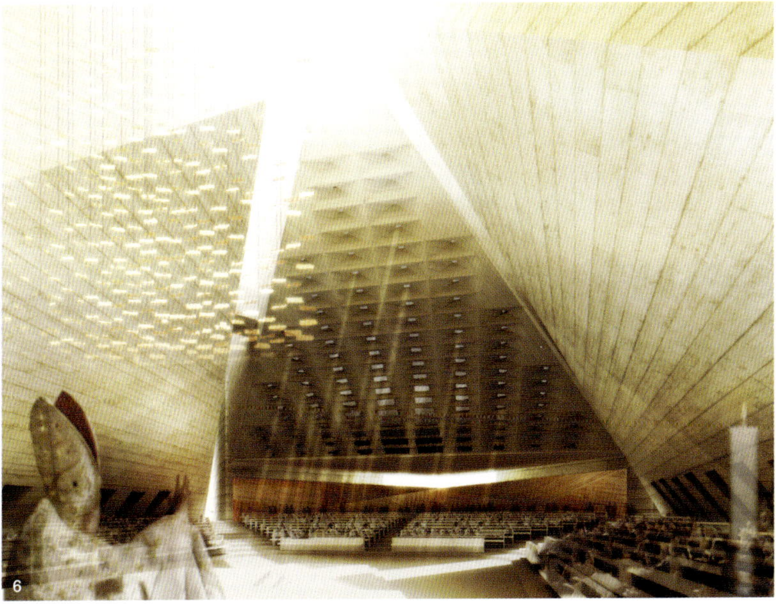
6

7

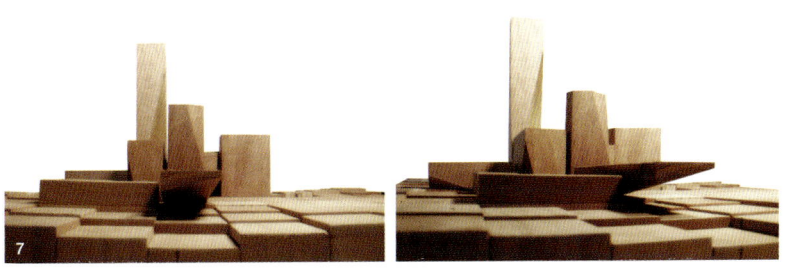

HSH South Harbour Master Plan
South Harbour, Helsinki, Finland, 2011

With nearly 180,000 islands, Finland is a country of unparalleled archipelagos and waterways. When viewed on a map, the country reveals a distinct pattern of islands and peninsulas that can be identified at different scales. Helsinki is no exception to this: the city is spread across a number of bays and islands that create a uniquely porous profile at its shores. Today, the city's South Harbor is one of the few coastal areas to have avoided this condition, making it an ideal site to restore the waterfront by deconstructing the existing port into a system of interconnected islands. This artificial archipelago will multiply the length of the waterfront and ensure maximum interaction between the water and public areas on the ground. Its structure of connected yet distinct elements allows similar activities to be clustered and connected together, while those that require more independence can be detached.

The success of a shorefront settlement frequently depends upon the quality of the urban edge that defines its interface with the water. Strengthening the relation between the city-structure and the sea means rethinking this border, creating an interlocking district between the city's edge and the sea. Our strategy does not try to insert a new iconic element at the waterfront; rather, it works with specific actions to strengthen the elements that have been overshadowed and neglected over time. The South Harbor proposal envisions three precise actions to efficiently reposition existing pieces within the city structure: bringing green space to the water's edge, activating open public spaces along the waterfront, and triggering new city-related activities within the marine space.

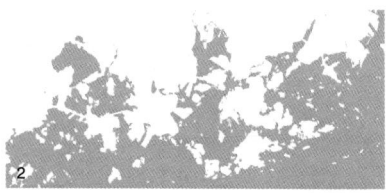

1: Finland archipelagos
2: Helsinki archipelagos
3: Overall view

4: Site rendering
5: Figure-ground plan with islands

6: New islands
7: Open spaces structure

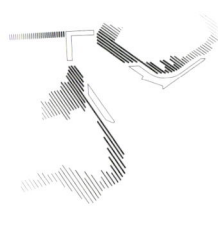

5

6

7

8: Site rendering
9: Existing waterfront

10: Urban grid structure
11: Proposed water structure

9   10   11

SOFTlab
Michael Szivos

Equity, Experimentation, and Failure

Work with "no precedent" is interesting because it is impossible. We always learn from and are influenced by what has been done before, reacting to our peers. SOFTlab is excited by the impossible; it fuels our desire, as designers, to erase what might be considered limits. As we discover how a brief or problem might be unique, we often start by looking at what it is not, to discover what it can become. We examine reality and the status quo in an effort to discover impossibility.

But without a precedent, how can we test ideas? Testing has become a crucial part of our practice, performed through a mix of research and ideas. In an effort to push back against the status quo, we embrace experimentation as a valuable mechanism for testing new ideas. We do not see experimentation as an interesting part of the studio; rather, we see it as a circumstance of how we operate. For experimentation to become a legitimate part of the studio we have accepted failure as integral to how we test ideas, prototypes, and methods. The acceptance of failure has resulted in an unexpected freedom in our work. The tendency for experimentation to be simply used as a descriptive term in design strips it of all of its liberating qualities. In this case a predetermined style is associated with experimentation to support a history of success. We are not interested in guarantees, especially their capacity to undermine experimentation. At the end of the day we are not interested in success; instead we are interested in doing great work and to do that we will have to fail.

In order to fully deromanticize experimentation we are trying to commodify it and turn it into a product. Can equity be associated with experimentation? How can something that accepts failure as inevitable be valuable? In our efforts to test solutions, failure produces such a degree of learning that the two words are sometimes interchangeable. It is through learning that experimentation produces equity for the studio. We would rather market our studio through this attitude and culture than through a style. "No precedent" implies looking at the past, but maybe it is the future that lacks precedent. We are lucky enough to be among peers who are very difficult to define, who stand out not by their difference, but by their attitudes. That is testimony to the precision at which they constantly evolve and adapt how they find, create, and imagine work. Maybe the concern is not relying on past precedents, but leaving behind no precedents.

CHROMAtex.me
New York, New York, 2010

CHROMAtex.me is a site-specific installation designed and produced by SOFTlab for the bridgegallery in New York. The installation was designed to produce a complex environmental and spatial combination of six colors. The color is mixed in the interior of the form, leaving a vibrant interior that is backlit by the gallery. The piece is inverted spatially; the interior of photo-glossy ink-jet-printed paper is meant to look very precise, finished, and smooth, while the exterior is textured with an array of binder clips used to hold the piece together. Rather than having a finished facade or skin that hides the method of construction, we chose to invert this relationship. The first thing viewers see is the method of fabrication.

As viewers move around the piece they discover the finished effects produced by the construction, experiencing the interior through a series of portals designed to offer a specific glimpse into the piece, starting from the front of the gallery. The installation was not only designed with the interior of the gallery in mind but also responds to the street, drawing people in. The largest portal into the piece is attached to the front window of the gallery, completely obscuring the interior except for views in through the gallery's glass door. Viewers are invited to look into the colored interior, only to enter the gallery and see an all-white exterior textured in thousands of binder clips. It is this contrast that makes the portals into the piece so sensational.

The installation is made of over 4,000 laser-cut panels of photo ink-jet paper. Each panel is a unique shape and printed with a custom color. The panels are connected using over 17,000 binder clips. The shape is reinforced using a series of custom acrylic rings. The overall form is hung from the ceiling of the gallery and completely suspended in the space without touching the ground.

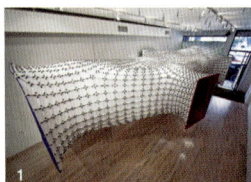

1: Exterior of the installation
2: Detail of the binder clips
3: View from below the piece

4: Exploded axonometric
5: The installation engages the street front.
6: Colored interior of the piece

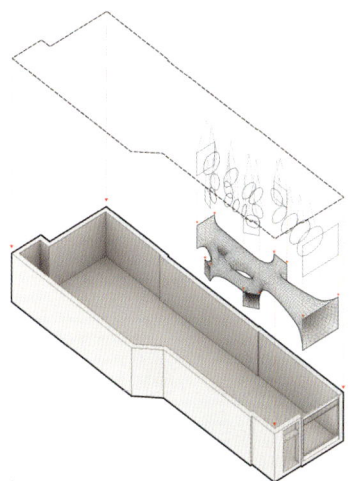
4

5

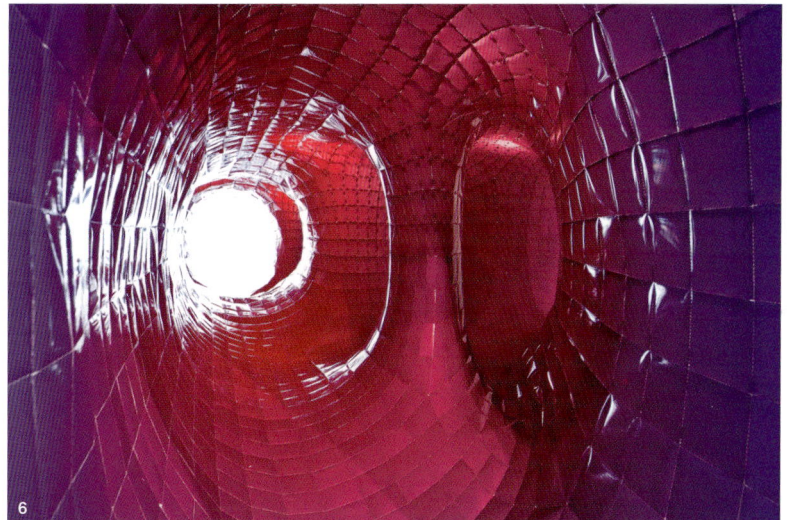
6

7: Sectional drawing
8: The overall installation
9: Another view from below
10: Aperture into the colored interior

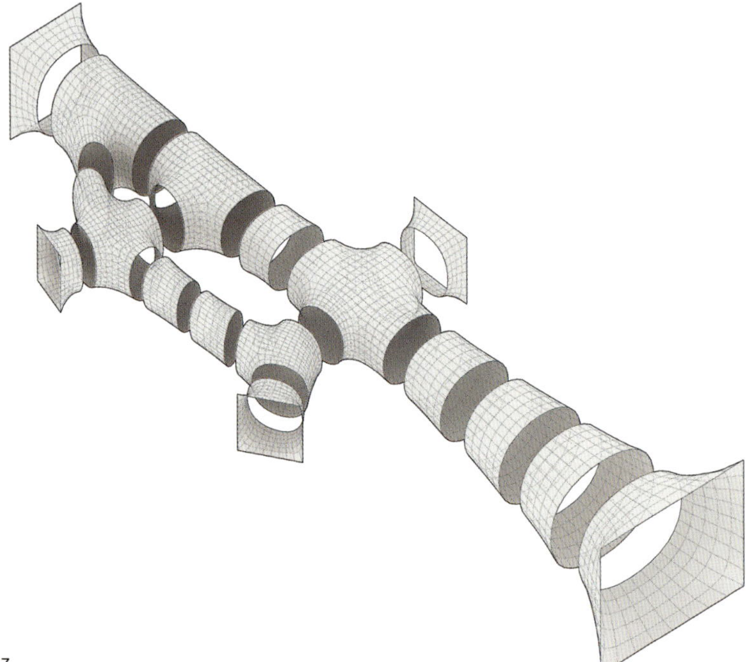

7

8

9

10

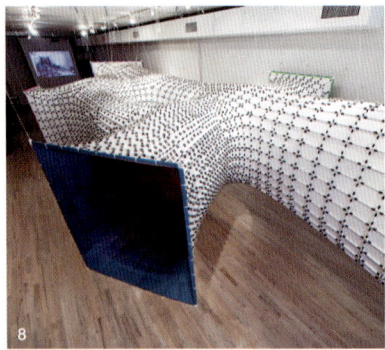

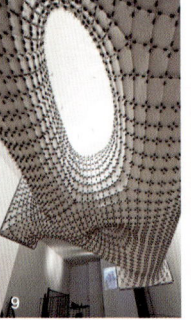

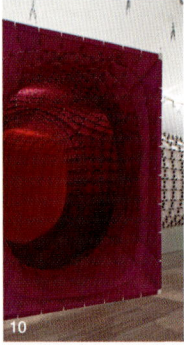

11: Colored interior of the piece

11

BOFFO Building Fashion 2011

New York, New York, 2011, with The Lake and Stars

Rather than thinking of our store as a pop-up or an installation, we conceived of it as a store within a store. We used the existing space to insert a store that amplifies one of the most basic mechanisms of retail, optics. The garments are displayed in a way that allows visitors to view specific details of the construction and form. The level of detail in the garments was amplified and/or multiplied through custom-built kaleidoscopic view cones. The view cones are covered in a matte-black tactile material that is soft to the touch and absorbs any extra light, showing preference to the vibrancy inside the viewing cones. The inside of the store is completely clad in a white glossy skin so it receives as much light from the viewing cones as possible. We used spotlights to shine focused light through the viewing cones to provide a multicolored kaleidoscopic light in the interior. As viewers move around the outside of the store and look through the viewing cones, they will block the focused light, causing the interior of the store to constantly shift in color and level of light. We subverted the traditional window display by only showing glimpses of the piece and using the curiosity of visitors to activate the space. In a way, we built a human-scale kaleidoscope of light and color that changes based on movement through the space. Rather than explicitly designing a color palette or specific form, we designed an apparatus that mapped—in real time—how people shop and interact with the garments.

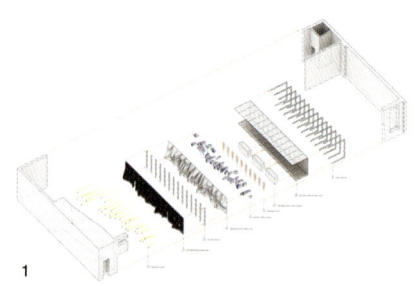

1

1: Exploded axonometric
2: Interior detail
3: Exterior wall

4: View cone
5: Exterior wall detail
6: Exterior wall

7: Elevation
8: Section detail

9: Custom hanger
10: View cone

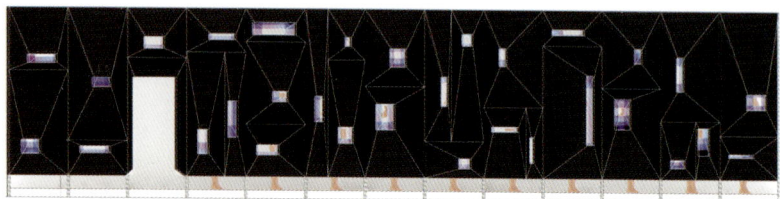

7

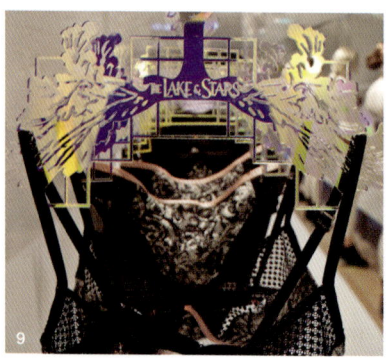

8

11: Interior

11

Shizuku
2009

This project represents a crossover of some of the various mediums we use and explore in the studio. We originally produced the short film *Shizuku* for the le:60 Film Festival in Boston, and curator Kelsey Harrington asked us to include it in a group exhibition at the Elga Wimmer Gallery in New York. The film includes live action video with camera-matched CG elements. For the exhibition we also produced a full-scale version of the CG elements to be displayed along with the video. The "drips" were made of laminated plywood sections and sanded to produce a smooth surface.

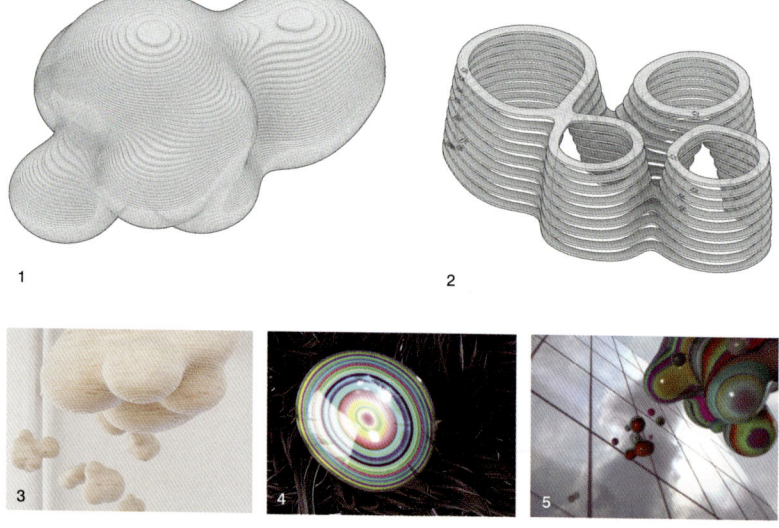

1

2

3

4

5

1: Layers
2: Layer assembly
3: Piece floating in the gallery

4–5: Video stills
6: Detail of the layered plywood construction
7: Piece from below

Let Us Make Cake

New York, New York, 2011

Let Us Make Cake was a collaborative video projection created by Nuit Blanche NY for the facade of the New Museum during the Festival of Ideas for the New City. We were asked to design one of the projections. Rather than create a completely digital video, we worked with Nuit Blanche to produce a piece that was more analog and relied on a physical scale model of the New Museum for production.

We decided to "light up" the museum by covering the facade with brightly colored tape. First, we produced a scale model of the museum and painted it black. We then filmed it at the angle and view of a pedestrian. The tape literally lights up the facade with strips of color. We purposely left in the shots with hands in front of the tape to add a strange, human scale to the piece and the idea that there is a larger set of hands controlling the appearance of the museum. This allusion to museums becoming more bureaucratic and protocol-driven might be a good thing. Rather than getting rid of protocols, we wanted to try inverting and streamlining them to make the museum more transparent and vibrant, to take advantage of the commodification of art and the museum rather than criticizing it.

1–2: Production of scale model
3: Projection of live video on the facade of the New Museum

4–5: Production stills

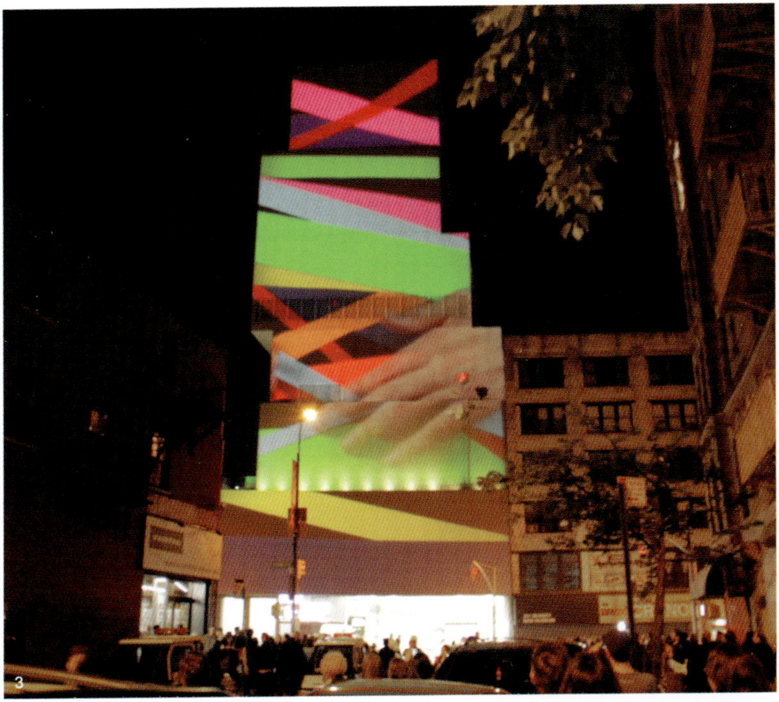

3

4

5

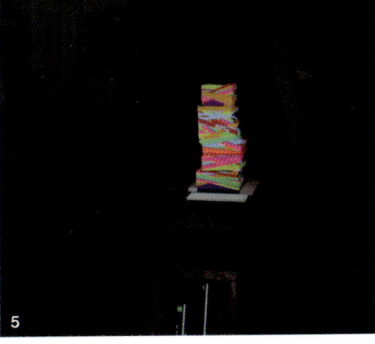

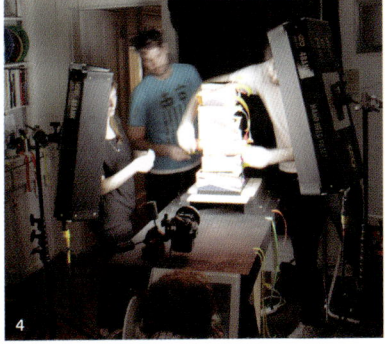

Blue Marlin

New York, New York, 2009

An industrial design and packaging company approached us to design a flex space for their offices. The space was to be used by clients for meetings as well as to house flexible work areas for clients working from their office. Blue Marlin's main concerns were keeping the space adaptable and encouraging creativity.

We designed and fabricated many of the elements of the renovation. The space included a storage wall made of cardboard tubes of varying sizes, custom light fixtures, and various furniture elements. A screen wall made of panels rotating at different angles produced a gradual pattern of transparency that allowed visitors to view more of the office as they entered the reception area. The overall space was subdivided by a series of rails and temporary walls made of industrial felt. The space could be used with an open plan or it could be divided into multiple configurations by moving the felt panels along the rails.

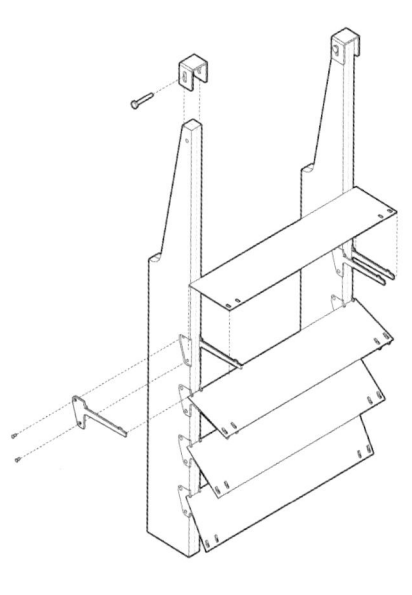

1

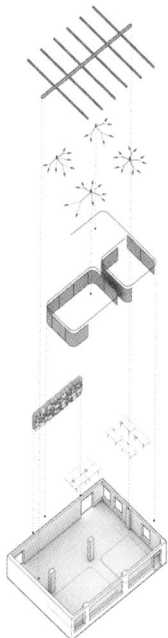

2

1: Screen wall detail
2: Exploded axonometric

3–**4**: Screen wall
5: Screen wall prototypes

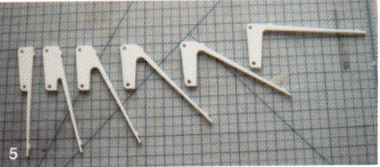

6: Felt curtain diagram
7–8: Flexible conference area

9: Conference area
10: Work area

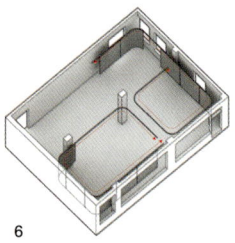 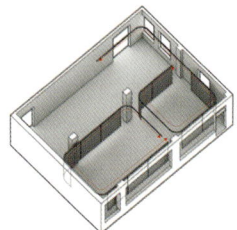 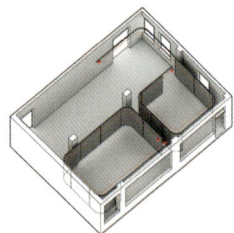

6

11–12: Storage wall

R&D:azzle
Brooklyn, New York, 2011

R&D:azzle was produced for the Creators Project: New York 2011, an art and technology festival created through a partnership between Vice and Intel. The two structures are made of plywood panels zip-tied together. The geometry is completely held together by the zip ties. There is no frame and the triangulation provides not only an irregular surface, but also a stable combination of points for each piece to rest on.

In an effort to have viewers engage with a static object, SOFTlab has designed an installation that is defined by impossible views. The piece is graphically camouflaged so that the shape is discovered by viewers as they move around the piece. The interior of the piece is an inversion of the exterior. While the exterior uses a disguise as camouflage, the interior uses a hyper version of its surroundings, employing the environment to confound visitors. The piece acts as an irregular kaleidoscope of color and light to produce fractured images of views that are irregular and at best impossible.

1: Exterior showing the striped patterning
2–**3**: Visitors interacting with the piece
4: The pieces are lit from within.

5: Cutout for viewing the interior;
panels are made of dichroic acrylic

pAlice

Brooklyn, New York, 2009

pAlice is one of our first environmental installations. The piece connects all of the openings in the room to a single surface, turning it inside out and giving viewers a reference to the exterior of the room without physical access to it. When viewers look inside the room they see a space that is defined by a surface formed from the connection of these openings without actually seeing the interior space of the room. Once viewers are inside the room, the geometry of the piece is visually camouflaged through a cladding of reflective panels. Unlike the exterior of the room, which is hidden by the interior of the piece, the interior of the room is mapped onto the piece through the reflective surface.

The piece was a chance to experiment with some of the research we had been developing in the studio regarding the automation of drawings for digital fabrication. This research is very much an ongoing part of the studio and we continue to implement it in many of our projects.

pAlice is made of over 2,400 laser-cut triangles and over 3,600 custom connections. All of the tooling and labeling was automated using a custom-written script for Maya.

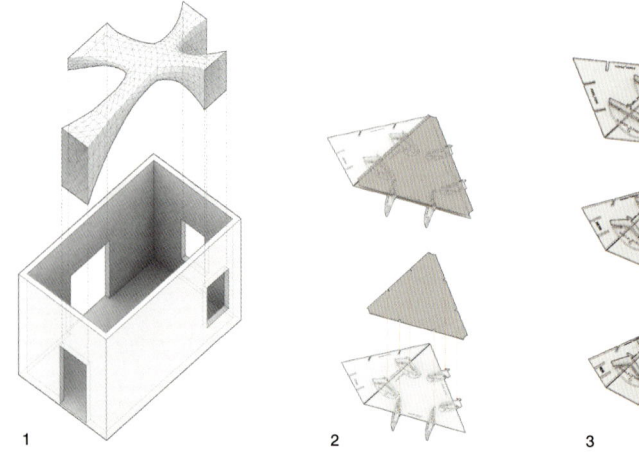

1   2   3

1: Exploded axonometric
2–3: Panel detail
4: Interior of the piece showing the custom joints
5: View from entrance

6: Reflective Mylar skin
7: Installation before Mylar skin
8: Skin panel detail
9: View from below

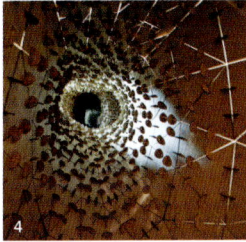

Xtra Moenia
New York, New York, 2011

Xtra Moenia is a site-specific installation designed and produced by SOFTlab for the San Gennaro North Gate. The piece was commissioned by Two Bridges Neighborhood Council and produced by the They Co. The piece serves as the North Gate to the annual Feast of San Gennaro festival in Little Italy. We developed a form created out of two distinct oculi as a reference to one of the simplest and most effective classical architecture devices. One oculus points up while the other hangs down, defining a zone on the street for pedestrians. The two forms are created using a minimal surface, blending the two oculi together in a way that blurs the distinction between the two. The final geometry was developed closely with the structural engineering firm Arup. The piece is completely held in tension from cables attached to the surrounding buildings. The shape is completely site specific and can only find its true form when attached at these specific points and tensioned with the proper lengths. Each piece is different, requiring custom software tools to be developed to fabricate the installation.

Extra Moenia is made of 4,224 laser-cut panels. Each panel is a unique shape and printed with a custom color. The panels are connected using over 6,000 aluminum grommets. The shape is held in complete tension using a complex system of cables and tubes attached to the surrounding buildings.

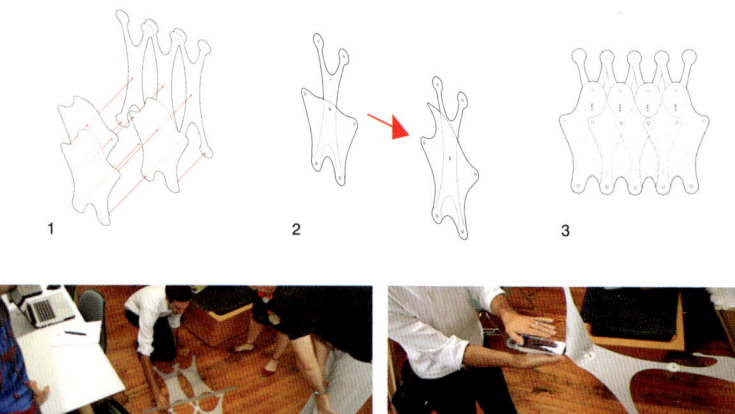

1   2   3

1: The color is generated through an overlap of translucent films.
2: Panel detail
3: The overlap between each panel is unique.

4–5: Material tests
6: View from above
7: The panels connecting the two oculi have a precisely distributed color variation.

8: Transition from one oculus to the other
9: Upper view toward the Puck Building

10: Color distribution
11–12: View from above

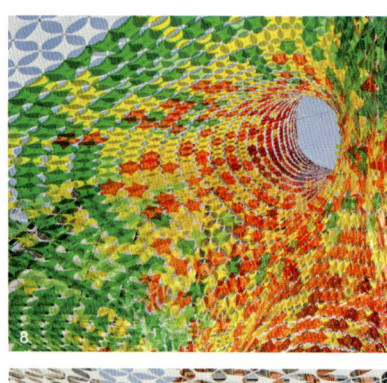

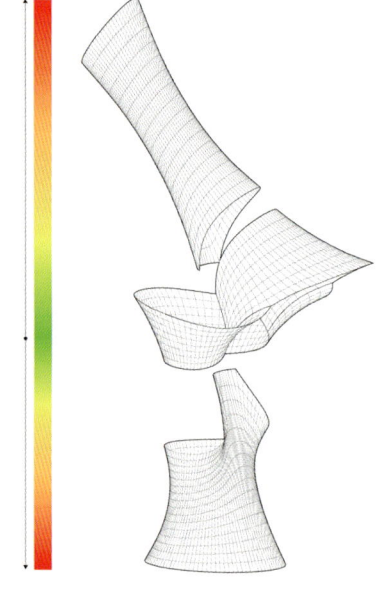

10

11

12

13: Lower ring

13

stpmj
Seung Teak Lee / Mi Jung Lim

Another Constraint

The unprecedented follows the unforeseen constraint.

There are many differences between the precedent and the unprecedented—different forms, systems, and programs, and even different eras—but the most easily identified is the addition of a new formal or theoretical constraint. Until recently, designers have relied on their complex and rapidly changing environments to generate spectrums of constraint. We identify one specific type, we call it "Another Constraint," a new perspective, built from careful observations of the social, political, environmental, structural, and economic phenomena of our time.

The intentional introduction of Another Constraint, something that has not been considered before, is our starting point for pursuit of the unprecedented. It fundamentally affects our methods of thinking, drawing, and construction. It multiplies possible solutions and pushes us forward.

Naturally, that which is unprecedented is ultimately assimilated and becomes, through time, constraint. Our solution is process, not product, and we see the unprecedented in architecture and its environment as the result of continually embracing Another Constraint.

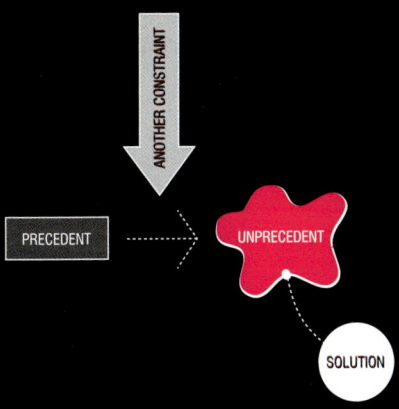

Rocking Sukkah

Toronto, Ontario, Canada, 2011

A chair surrounded by an extremely slender, 24-foot-tall bamboo lattice that is light, flexible, and strong, Rocking Sukkah is made of two main components—a bamboo screen and a platform. The platform consists of a convex circular base and an armchair, both built from CNC-cut plywood. The rest of the plywood is chopped and placed in the base's gap. This debris gives the base a low center of mass and provides the rest of the structure with kinetic freedom. It prevents the structure from tipping over, even while occupied. The bamboo screen comprises 90 percent of the total structure, but it is light, weighing only 80 pounds. Bamboo diameters taper from 1¼" at the bottom to ¼" at the top, keeping the structure's center of gravity under 8' from ground level.

Rocking Sukkah is a playful, interactive single-occupancy space, where the user can control the sukkah's movement based on their desired orientation toward the sun or the stars. As the bottom rotates, the top moves in a larger circumference, creating dramatically animated motions during both day and night. The sukkah responds not only to the user's movement but also, when unoccupied, to wind currents.

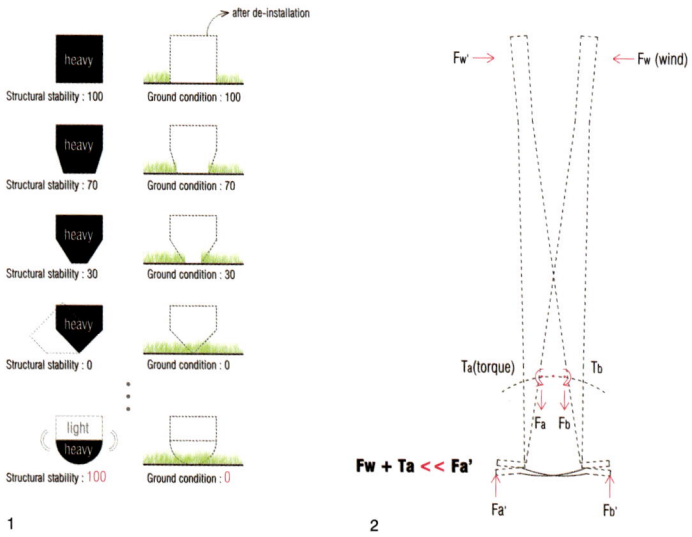

1

2

1: Structure and ground condition diagram
2: Structural performance diagram

3: Installation on grass
4: Elevation / various bamboo diameters

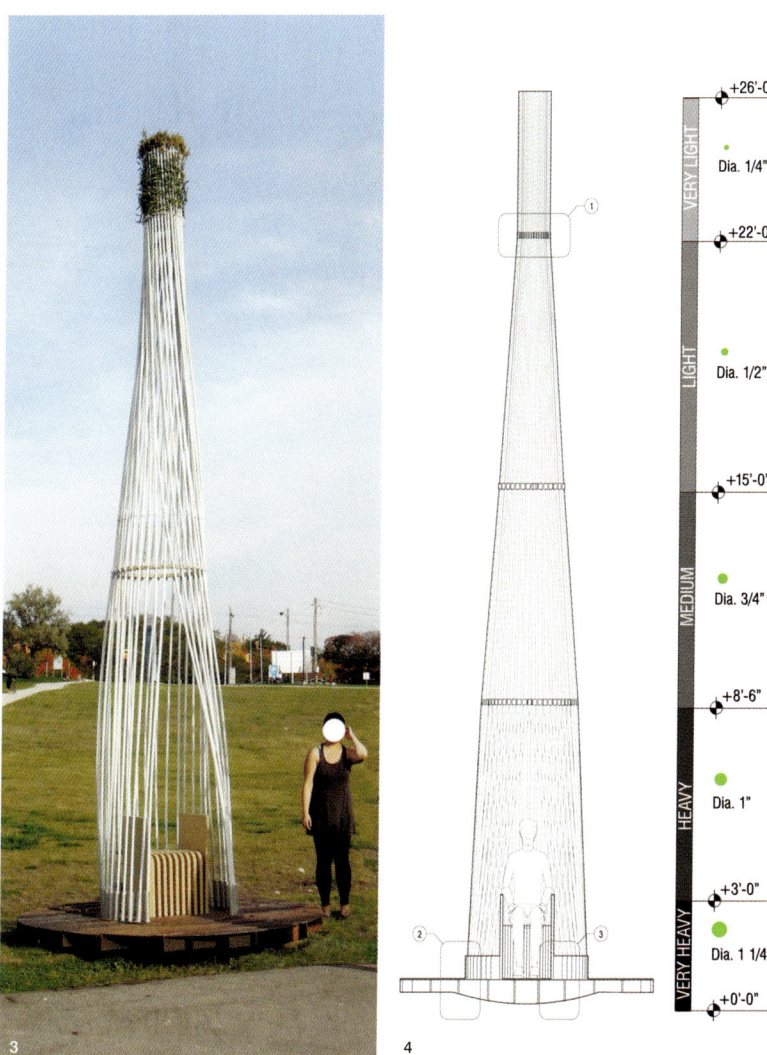

+26'-0"

VERY LIGHT

• Dia. 1/4"

+22'-0"

LIGHT

• Dia. 1/2"

+15'-0"

MEDIUM

● Dia. 3/4"

+8'-6"

HEAVY

● Dia. 1"

+3'-0"

VERY HEAVY

● Dia. 1 1/4"

+0'-0"

5: Rocking operation at daytime

6: The structure glows at night.

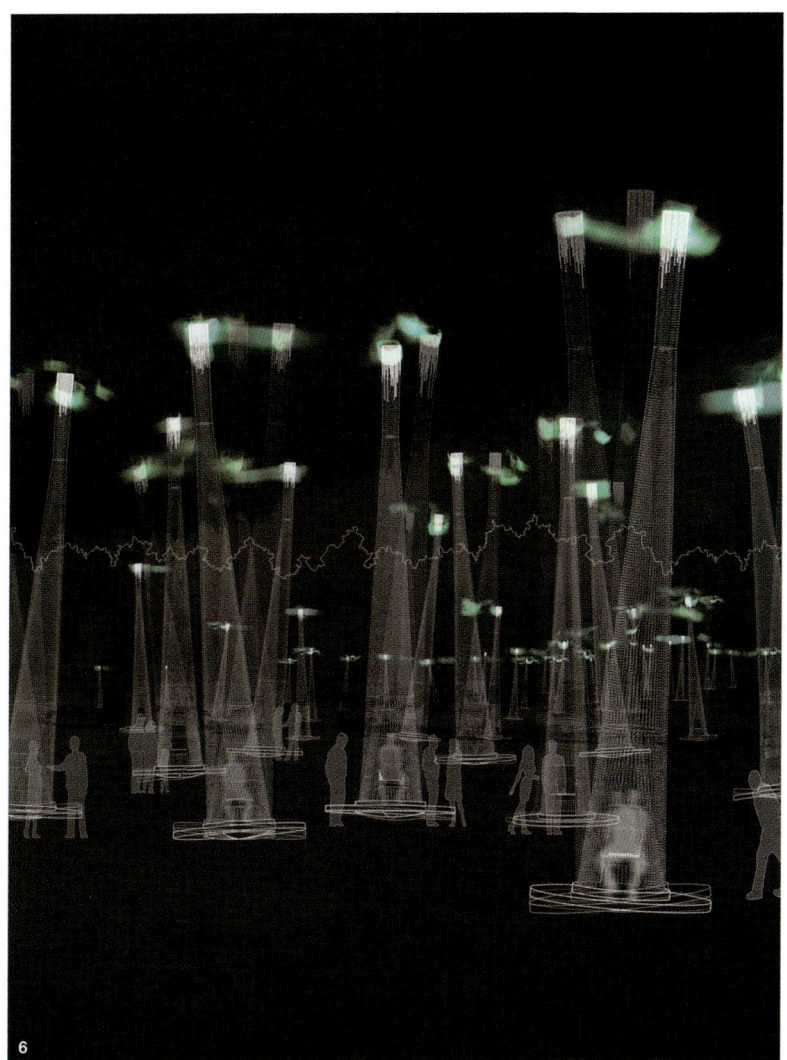

6

Amphisteps
Salt Lake City, Utah, 2010

Amphisteps is a new type of urban amphitheater where cultural events like film festivals and street performances can happen spontaneously. In order to meet such distinct needs for the site, the project provides two configurations through the assembly of lightweight components that allow people to change positions easily. Each seating block is simply reclaimed bluefoam sandwiched between plywood sheets by thin wire braces. The volume of foam minimizes the weight of the block. The staggered-stacking bluefoam reduces the volume to 60 percent, keeping the structure stable. Two or three people can easily prepare and move the block for transport, installation, and reconfiguration.

It consists of twelve triangular prisms, each oriented differently. The prisms can connect a small audience to a single stage / screen or multiple stages so the audience can experience many performances simultaneously. While climbing the steps, visitors enjoy tempos and rhythms from changing directions, and choose the performances they want to watch. Traversing the steps becomes a sort of cultural hike.

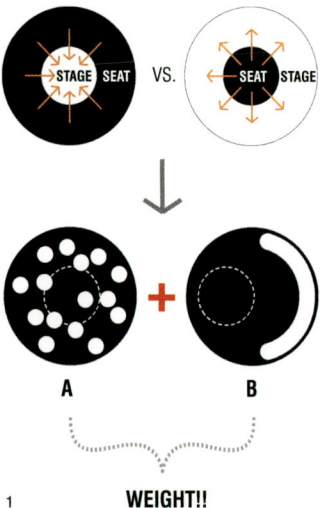

1

2

1: Seat and stage diagram

2: Bluefoam stacked-step block

3: Configuration A for street performances

4: Configuration B for a film projection

3

4

Parallelogrammic Hou(s)tation

Competition winning entry, 2011

Parallelogrammic Hou(s)tation is a new suburban type demanded by the change of transportation mode, from car to high-speed rail. It is proposed as an alternative to twentieth-century suburban development, especially the negative impact of its automobile-centered design and related requirements such as parking spaces, heavy highway interchanges, traffic congestion, and increased CO_2 emissions.

The project combines the benefits of both urban and suburban life. Located within a one-hour high-speed-train ride of two major cities, it will provide nearby residents with proximate access to both metropolises. The side length of the Hou(s)tation is defined by the length of the high-speed train and the number of cars. Each car drops residents and visitors on discreet lobby platforms that offer easy access to individual houses and centrally located public program areas. A train's car numbers are used to designate streets as part of the wayfinding system; passengers would take the car appropriate to their street. The Hou(s)tation, bounded by the railway and perimeter green buffer, allows for more compact infrastructures, a greater reduction in energy consumption, and more efficient land use. It minimizes air pollution and negative environmental impacts, and maximizes the surrounding nature.

High-speed rail becomes a part of the house
The house becomes a part of the station
The station becomes a part of the town
The town becomes a part of the landscape

1: Perspective
2: Enlarged plan
3: A single Hou(s)tation

4: Future growth of Hou(s)tation
5: New landscape of Hou(s)tation

Opera'S'

Busan, South Korea, 2011

Opera'S' proposes to use the central location of a complex site as a formative element to establish a cultural and waterfront beacon for Busan. Located on the water, the opera house is flanked by a 1,200-foot-high mountain, tall residential towers, the Busan rail station, and an international seaport. The opera house engages the context with various heights. The open exterior views from within the theater and an iconic flytower connect the theater to its rich urban context, punctuating a new cultural locus on the skyline of Busan.

As a new public icon, the elongated flytower serves multiple functional and conceptual purposes. As smoke from a factory chimney might serve as an icon of a city's industrial past, the flytower will serve as a cultural beacon for the city's future. The space and its functions—the mechanical movement of movable panel arrays, ceiling guided trusses, counterweights, scenery, and lighting of the auditorium are revealed and open for public view behind a transparent wall. The animation of these elements offers another opera to its high neighbors. The opera complex will serve as a cultural heart in this dense and varied urban environment, a visible beacon between the sea and land.

1: Aerial view with urban development
of the port city

2: Perspective looking toward city
3: Topography diagram

4: Main opera house A
5: Multipurpose theater B
6: Section model photo

Inside, stages A and B are provided with an operable, folding partition along the back wall to invite the cityscape's cinematic character into the space of the opera. Opera House A opens to the city, using the night skyline as an operatic backdrop, and multipurpose Theater B opens to the water, using the sea and horizon beyond as a backdrop.

6

7: Perspective at vertical street gallery
8: Exterior view at night

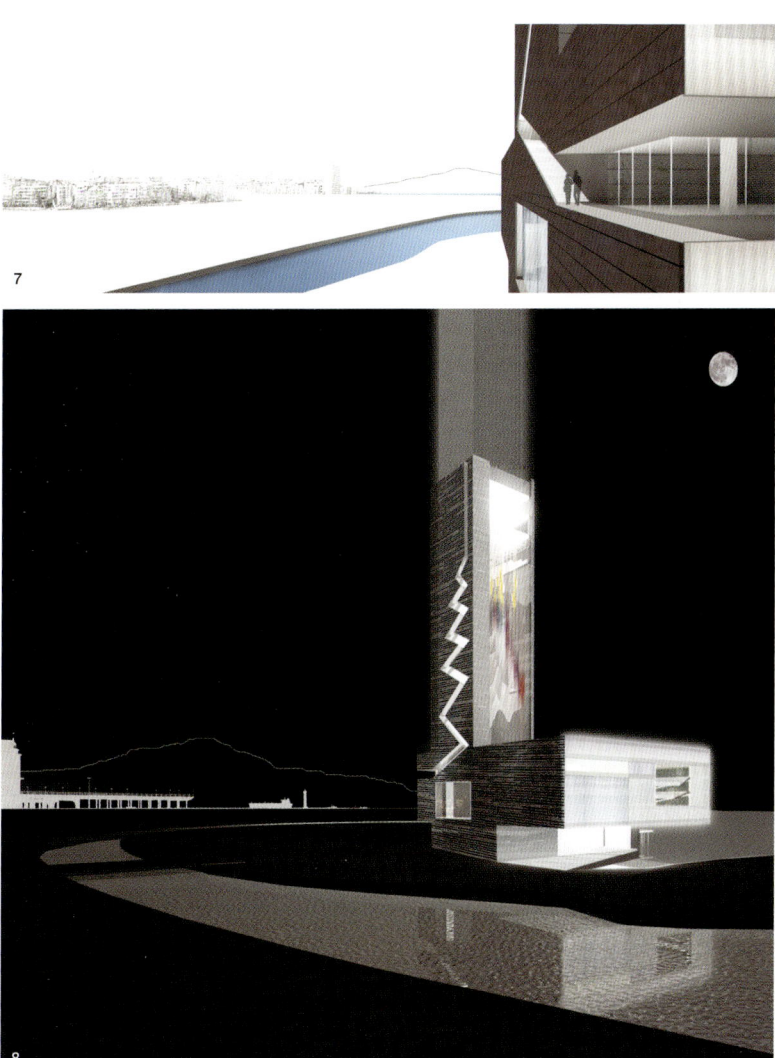

7

8

Performative Dryer
Governors Island, New York, 2011

Performative Dryer addresses two issues: the large amount of consumption and waste produced by laundry services in New York City, where an estimated 65 million wire hangers are discarded every year. The canopy provides a large, open main space for performances as well as smaller gathering spaces for visitors to bring and hang wet clothing. The wet laundry causes the structure to sag under the weight, but as it dries the structure slowly recovers its form, and the evaporative drying action cools the underside of the canopy. By making their own shades, visitors can enjoy a socially and culturally engaged picnic under the structure while their clothes dry. After the festival, the disassembled hanger units will be donated to neighbors, offering a cheap alternative to electric dryers. The Performative Dryer will disperse as the units travel throughout the city.

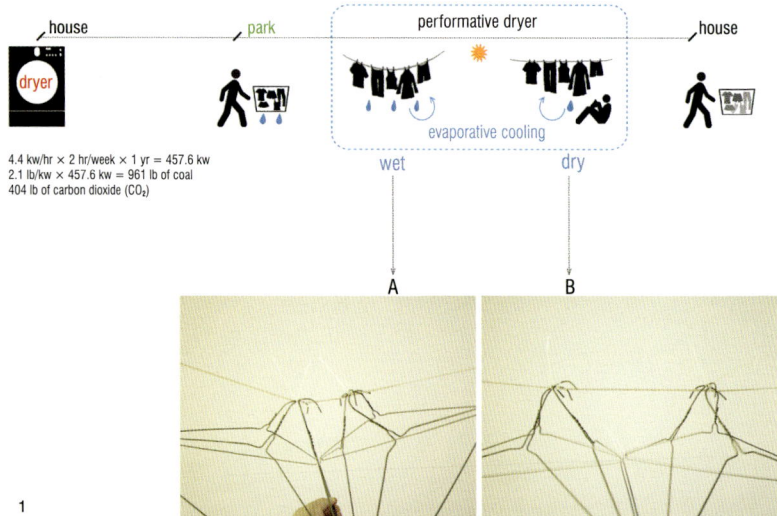

4.4 kw/hr × 2 hr/week × 1 yr = 457.6 kw
2.1 lb/kw × 457.6 kw = 961 lb of coal
404 lb of carbon dioxide (CO_2)

1

1: Evaporative cooling diagram
2: Section
3: Perspective

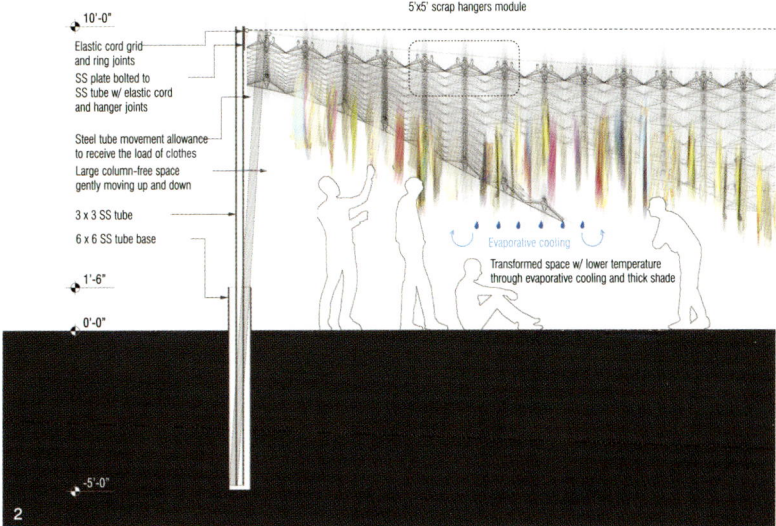

10'-0"

Elastic cord grid
and ring joints

SS plate bolted to
SS tube w/ elastic cord
and hanger joints

Steel tube movement allowance
to receive the load of clothes

Large column-free space
gently moving up and down

3 x 3 SS tube

6 x 6 SS tube base

1'-6"

0'-0"

-5'-0"

2

5'x5' scrap hangers module

Evaporative cooling

Transformed space w/ lower temperature
through evaporative cooling and thick shade

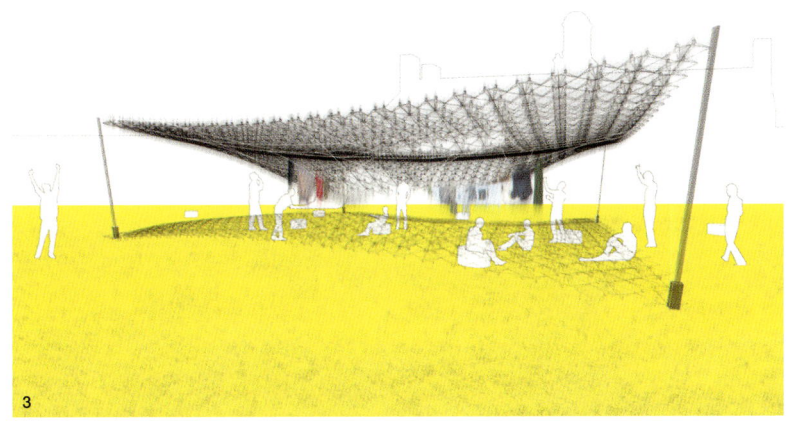

3

n! McCormicks

Chicago, Illinois, 2011

n! McCormicks is a linked set of eclectic programs built on twelve detached structures near McCormick Place's existing east building. Maintaining the Arie Crown theater element, the existing building is divided into twelve smaller pieces based on an existing 150' × 150' column grid. These squares are scattered on the lake, blurring any simple distinctions between land, water, and building.

The goal was to drastically increase the amount of exposed surface area to the water and provide multiple opportunities to experience the water through a variety of programs, transportation systems, and renewable energy schemes. Additionally, the project expands the current site boundary horizontally and vertically by forming an integrated loop system connecting new programs with McCormick Place and Northerly Island Park. Each new program sits on scrapped barges or inflatable tubes and responds to the flow of water, creating a kinetic visual dialogue between units. Repurposed old roof structures form a new ground on the floating archipelago. When viewed from the city at a distance, the various programs appear to coalesce into a single unit, slowly rotating on the lake.

1

1: Aerial view from airship
2: Sustainability diagram
3: Postcard from the future

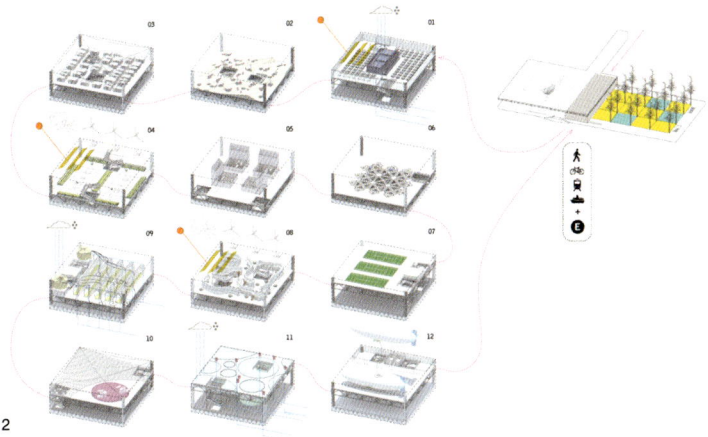

2

3

Switch On & On
Competition finalist, 2010

Conceived as a two-sectioned hybrid house, Switch On & On combines distinct thermal conditions to minimize energy consumption. The "platform" section provides a protective thermal enclosure and functional spaces for colder seasons. We designed the "floating" section using lightweight, prefabricated components with a passive cooling system, optimized for the summer season. This configuration responds to extreme climate shifts with simple and logical divisions of the house's energy systems.

The project expands and contracts with changing temperatures. To conserve energy, inhabitants will choose to live mostly in the platform house during cold seasons. This thermal zone is protected with thick insulation and heated mostly by passive means, including radiant heating in the floor slab and a green roof. During warm seasons, inhabitants will migrate up to the floating house, which offers natural shade of rooftop vegetation. The floating house is passively cooled in multiple ways, including through the back terrace and courtyard, and even by a swinging shutter with overhanging windows. This approach will maintain temperatures in both houses at an approximately 30 percent differential between the inside and outside during each season.

1

1: Floor plans
2–3: Model
3: Section

2

3

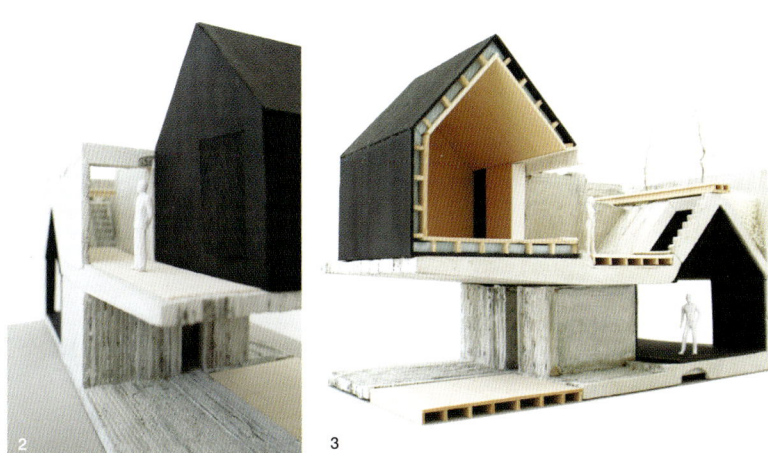

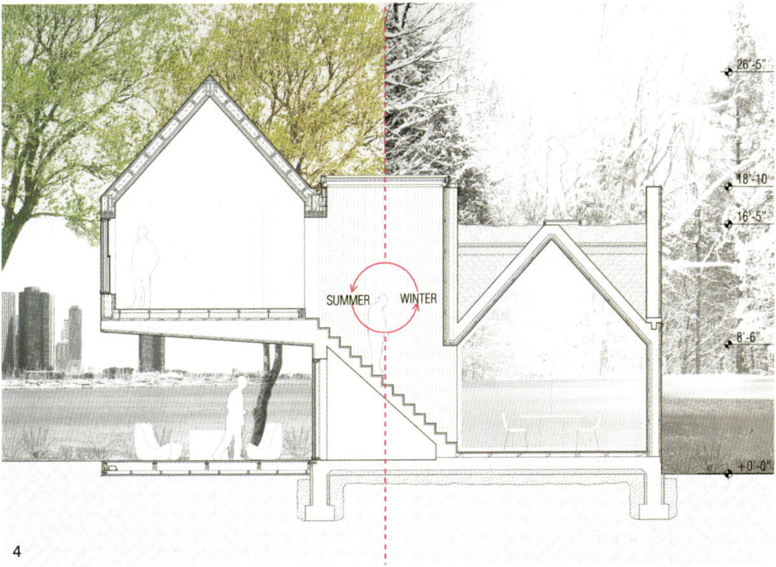
26'-5"
18'-10
16'-5"
SUMMER
WINTER
8'-6"
+0'-0"

4

Bungee to the Scar
Chicago, Illinois, 2010

In the city of Chicago, a 150-story condominium tower had stalled during its foundation construction because of the Great Recession, physically leaving a big scar on the city. Normally the form reflects the program, or becomes molded to it as it is developed, but in this project, the leftover form demanded an alternative program. Instead of modifying the massive foundation hole for a new usage or plan, we left it as is and proposed to transform it into a temporary bungee recreation park until such a time as construction could resume. With this simple and economically sensitive proposal, the foundation pit, the urban scar, becomes a unique public space.

The hole is surrounded by a tapered inflatable wall and a steel truss structure sits on the concrete rims of each sublevel floor in the hole. The moduled steel bars support circulation and carry multiple bungee stations that are placed at various heights. The bungee park can be readily disassembled so that the originally planned tower can resume. The disassembled inflatable wall and steel bars will be reassembled into a pavilion, a gallery, or even an above-ground bungee jump structure in the neighboring park, where it will stand as a souvenir of the Great Recession.

1: Aerial view of site

2: Perspective at bottom of hole

3: Perspective at top of hole

4: Sectional perspective with postcrisis use

Programmed Megacore
Seoul, South Korea, 2011

Postcrisis eras such as we are currently experiencing are unique times that offer architects profound opportunities to rethink and redefine the field. We are constantly asked to be more timely and cost-effective, and the Programmed Megacore suggests a new type of urban development.

The site is an entire district in Seoul, six individual buildings that include an office, residential tower, hotel, theater, retail space, and gallery. These buildings' cores are not efficient due to the different core occupancy rates on weekdays, weekends, mornings, and evenings. The proposal is to combine these dramatically different cores into one shared megacore.

The megacore supports several different programs. It takes advantage of the inner space by adding windowless program spaces like large theaters, museums, gyms, and retail spaces. The window-based programs (the office, residential, and hotel space) are placed on the perimeter of the core. This approach radically reduces the existing ratio of the floor area to core area and provides financial opportunities by creating more spaces for commercial occupancy.

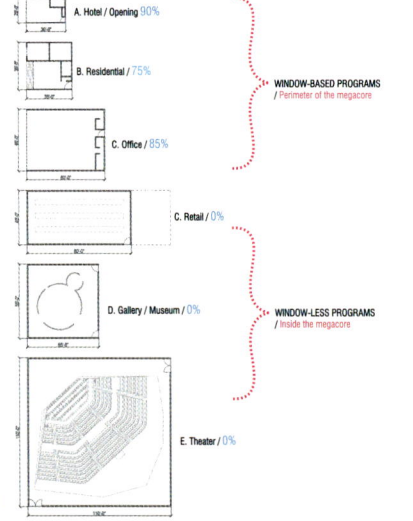

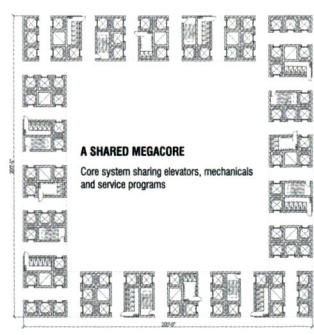

1

2

1: Typical dimensions and opening areas
2: Megacore plan
3: Exploded rendering of combined programs

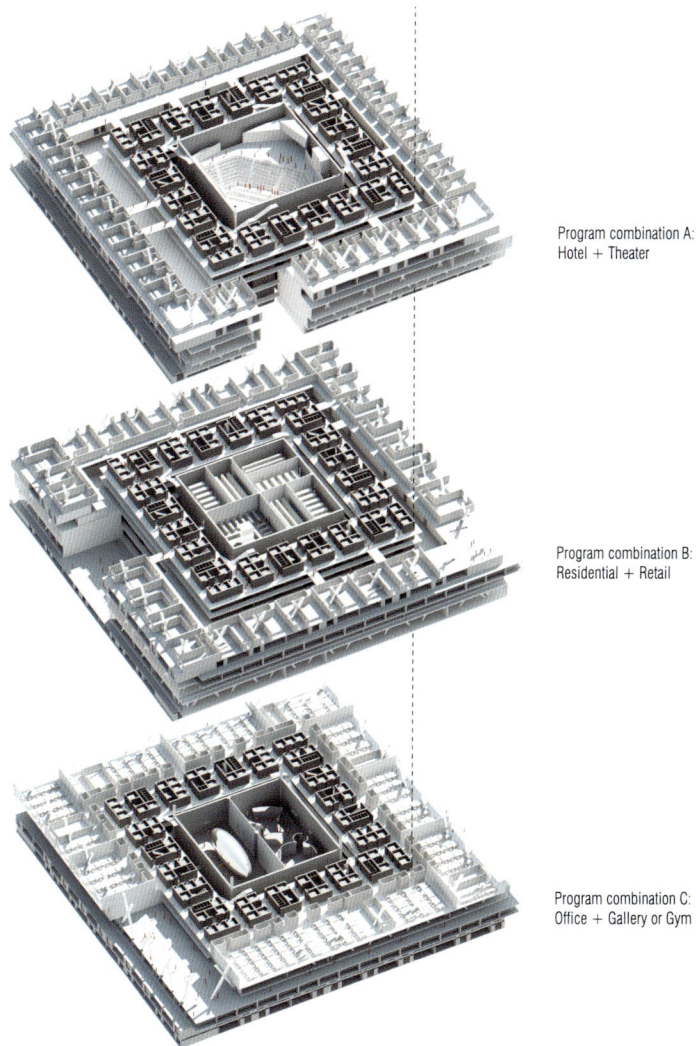

Program combination A:
Hotel + Theater

Program combination B:
Residential + Retail

Program combination C:
Office + Gallery or Gym

3

Synaesthetic Sense

Gwang Ju Design Biennale, with Korean GSD team, 2009

A Korean *soswaewon* (traditional garden) provides diverse experiences for visitors. The typical soswaewon provides visual corridors through a surrounding forest, incorporates different types of natural ventilation, and features a constant play of light and shadow amid the sounds of rustling bamboo. These experiences create an emotional atmosphere unique to soswaewon, which closely ties the senses to the micronature of the garden.

The Synaesthetic Sense installation is a borderless field of five hundred metal coil springs laid out in different numerical coordinates, each with its own length. The coil spring becomes an interactive medium possessing constantly changing surface and volume, providing opportunities for people to explore changing relationships between force, sound, and transparency as they pass through.

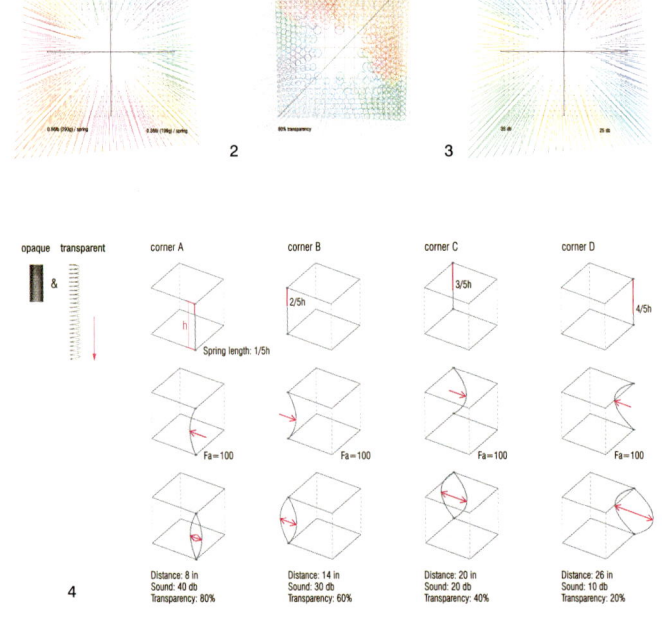

1: Visualized tension at plan
2: Visualized transparency at plan
3: Visualized pitch of sound at plan
4: Distributed spring diagram

5: Top slab from below
6: Bottom slab from above
7: Installation

WEATHERS
Sean Lally

Sean Lally's architecture employs the energies within our surrounding environment—electromagnetic, thermodynamic, acoustic, and chemical—as innovative new building blocks, forgoing the walls and shells that some assume to be the only type of architecture. Lally's designs develop their own shapes, aesthetics, organizational systems, and social experiences through a range of material energies that share the physical properties of the surrounding environment. In doing so, energy becomes more than what fills the interior of buildings or reflects off its outer walls. It becomes its own enterprise for design innovation: it becomes architecture itself.

The body of work presented here is rooted in the belief that architects possess the ability not only to harness the latest technologies and advancements in building materials but also to execute their imagination, projecting worlds and environments that will come to pass. The work shows that some of the greatest discoveries come not from seeking something new, but from reimagining what surrounds us.

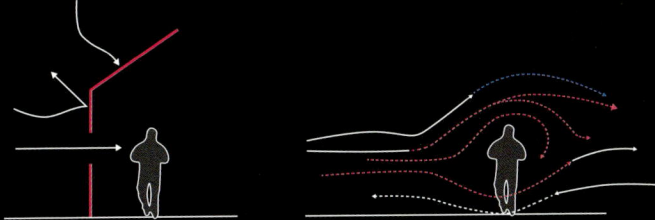

Architecture as an act of *mediation* vs. architecture as an *active context*

Sirenuse

Installation proposal, Chicago, Illinois, 2011, with Thomas Kelley

Sirenuse is a proposal for an exterior space that attracts people and activities during Chicago's late fall and winter months, a time when the place would be otherwise unusable. The mound itself and surrounding grounds engage visitors beyond simple body ergonomics (options for seating and reclining), and instead enhance the site's climate and the body's sensory perception through temperature regulation, varied lighting, and acoustics. These "sensorial envelopes" of the human body inform spatial organization by detecting the material energies that make up the local environment.

Sirenuse is more than an urban oasis; it creates space and activities that suspend the need for either walls or canopies. It offers a new definition of space, subverting the dichotomy of landscape and architectural form using material energies to define spatial boundaries and shape.

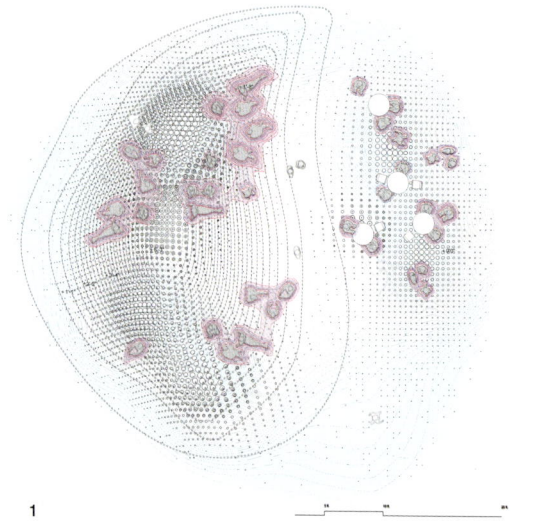

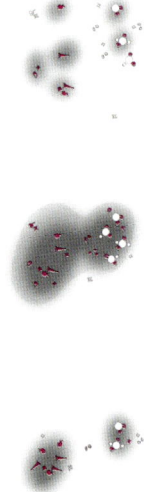

1   2

1: Plan
2: Spatial typologies: dispersed,
continuous, and groupings

3: View of tactile mound and seating,
physical model

3

4–5: Physical model

6: Sensorial envelopes:
The human body's sensorial perception defines
personal envelopes that can inform spatial
organizations by detecting the material energies
that make up the local environment.

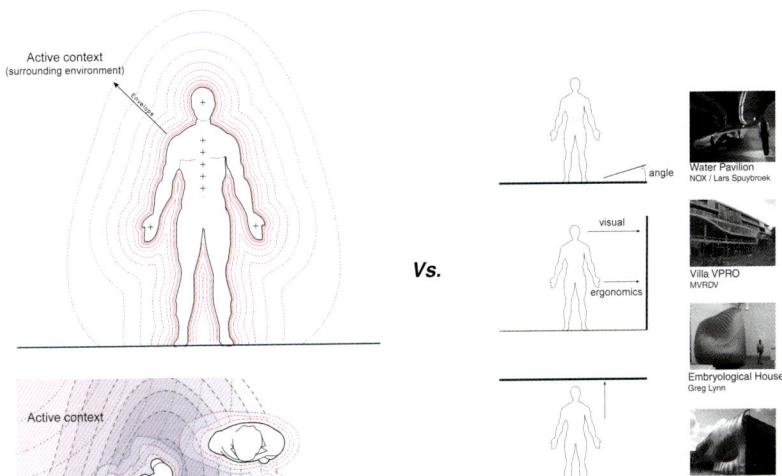

Active context
(surrounding environment)

Active context

Sensorial
Envelope

_Vs._

angle

Water Pavilion
NOX / Lars Spuybroek

visual

ergonomics

Villa VPRO
MVRDV

Embryological House
Greg Lynn

Maison Folie
NOX / Lars Spuybroek

Assumptions of Boundaries & Space

Active Context

+ Ambient Temperature
    Tactility (units)
    Conduction (units)

+ Light level
    Blue Spectrum
    Full Spectrum
    Red Spectrum

+ Olfactory

+ Sound
    Noise Cancelation
    Masking
    Vibration

6

Estonian Academy of Arts

Two-stage competition, Tallinn, Estonia, 2008
with Marina Nicollier, Viktor Ramos, John Carr, and Ali Naghdali
in collaboration with Morris Architects

The Estonian Academy of Arts asserts its identity and position within the city of Tallinn at both the level of the school's internal operations, and its contribution to the city's need for public spaces, including parks, garden space, galleries, and shops. In this proposal, a series of "artificial climatic lungs" separate the building into six zones and connect the elevated school to a public park below. The park itself is located on top of the school's primary mechanical systems and workshop, half a story off the street, capturing and amplifying the building's energy to sustain lush gardens throughout Estonia's long winters. The lungs also provide full-spectrum lighting to counteract the winter's shorter daylight hours. For close to a third of the year, light enters the building from the glass lungs below—the building's true facade. The lungs are organizational devices exposed to the external environment, but nested internally in the building envelope.

1

1: 1:500 scale model
2: The artificial climatic lungs, positioned between the floor plates above and public park below

3: Physical model, artificial climatic lungs moving through the building

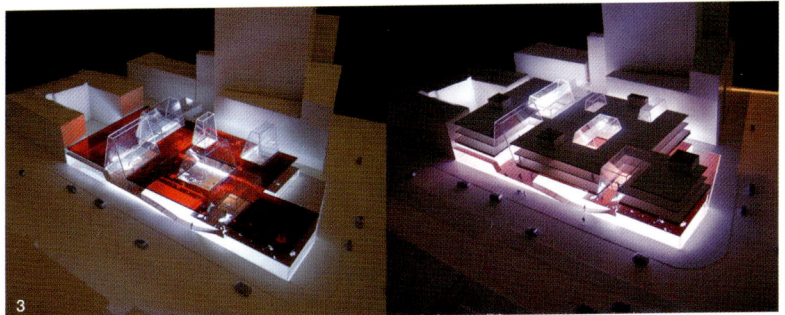

4: Point sources allow climate control, upper levels utilize climate zones below, and variations in climate control create distinct zones.

5: Interior perspective
6: Thermal section of artificially controlled garden and public spaces

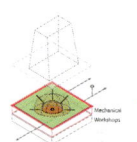 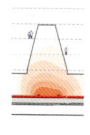 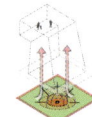 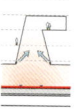 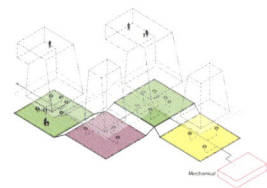

4

5

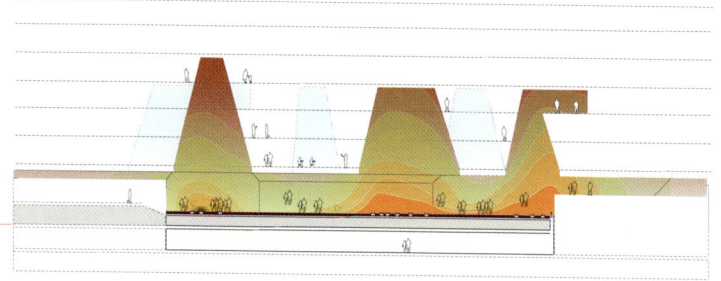

6

7: Project organization and systems

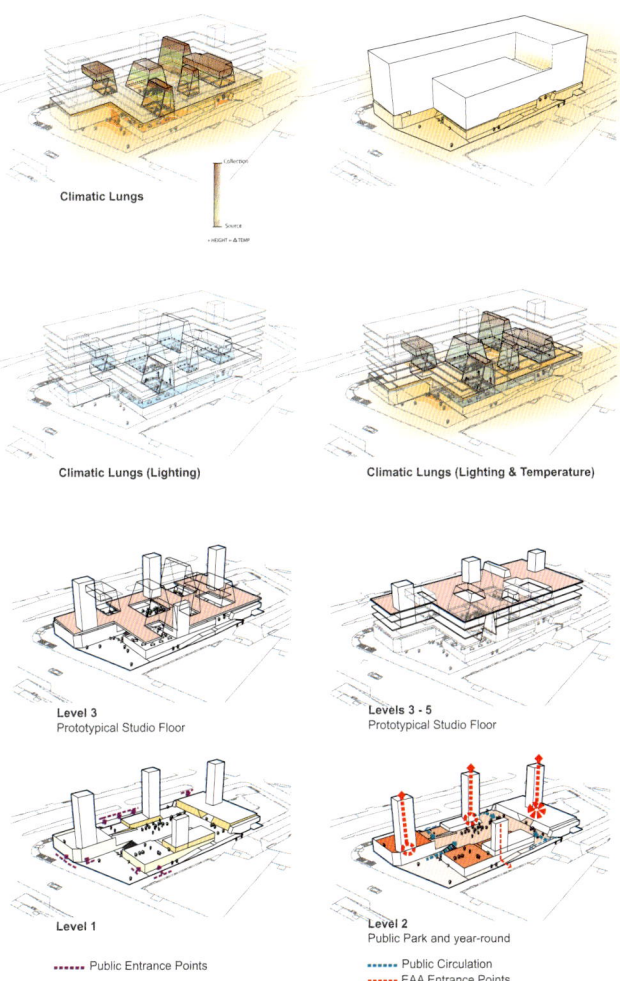

Climatic Lungs

Climatic Lungs (Lighting)

Climatic Lungs (Lighting & Temperature)

Level 3
Prototypical Studio Floor

Levels 3 - 5
Prototypical Studio Floor

Level 1

▪▪▪▪▪▪ Public Entrance Points

Level 2
Public Park and year-round

▪▪▪▪▪▪ Public Circulation
▪▪▪▪▪▪ EAA Entrance Points

Vatnsmyri Urban Planning

Competition entry, Reykjavik, Iceland, 2007
with Andrew Corrigan and Paul Kweton

Similar to the site's existing thermal pools, where ocean water mixes with recycled geothermally heated water to create unique swimming conditions all year round, the plan for Vatnsmyri will apply natural thermal resources to the climate conditions on land, including air and soil temperature to promote plant growth and usable outdoor spaces. Each of the proposed landforms around the site is tied to the others by a "climatic wash" that provides and controls the amenities needed to organize the city's development. Here, the climatic wash will extend the seasonal activities, control thermal variations in the soil and air, and extend usable outdoor time.

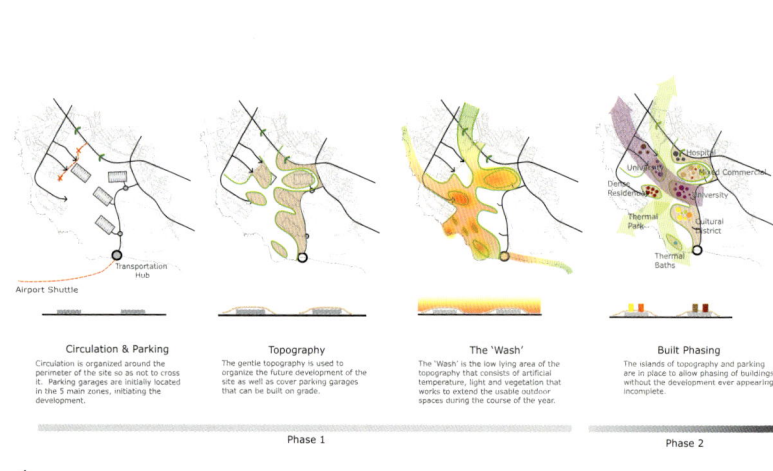

Circulation & Parking	Topography	The 'Wash'	Built Phasing
Circulation is organized around the perimeter of the site so as not to cross it. Parking garages are initially located in the 5 main zones, initiating the development.	The gentle topography is used to organize the future development of the site as well as cover parking garages that can be built on grade.	The 'Wash' is the low lying area of the topography that consists of artificial temperature, light and vegetation that works to extend the usable outdoor spaces during the course of the year.	The islands of topography and parking are in place to allow phasing of buildings without the development ever appearing incomplete.

Phase 1

Phase 2

1

1: Site organization and phasing
2: The climatic wash acts as connective tissue
between the north of the site and the south

3: Site view of the climatic wash

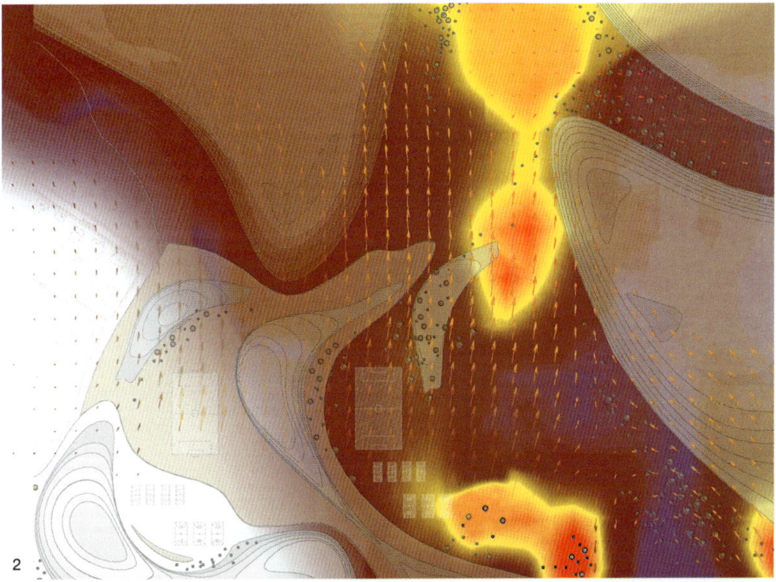

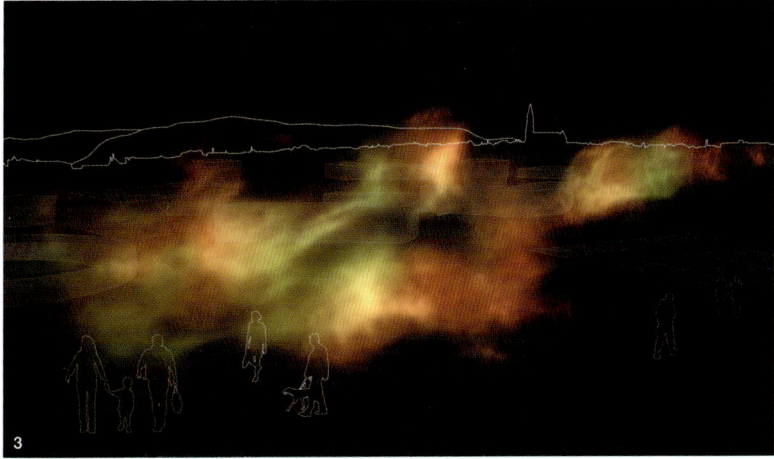

SHAGG

San Fernando Corridor Temporary Artwork, installation proposal, 2009–10
with Marina Nicollier and Matt Vander Ploeg

SHAGG picks up where Astroturf left off, creating an artificial carpet for the human body to engage in the exterior environment. No longer able to accept that the various energies within our environment are beyond our control, SHAGG attempts to design these energy systems and make them the new building blocks of architecture. The project creates an outdoor carpet-sized garden that does not rely on the sun's light for warmth and photosynthesis; its color and bloom are no longer tied to the seasons; and the distracting sounds of traffic and neighbors are overcome by white-noise emitters embedded under the 30,000-square-meter surface area. Composed of a series of strategically placed carpets that emit light, heat, and sound, SHAGG produces a level of artificial coziness, creating an environment that enables social gathering. Rather than try to re-create the recognizable, SHAGG is used to design its own microworlds.

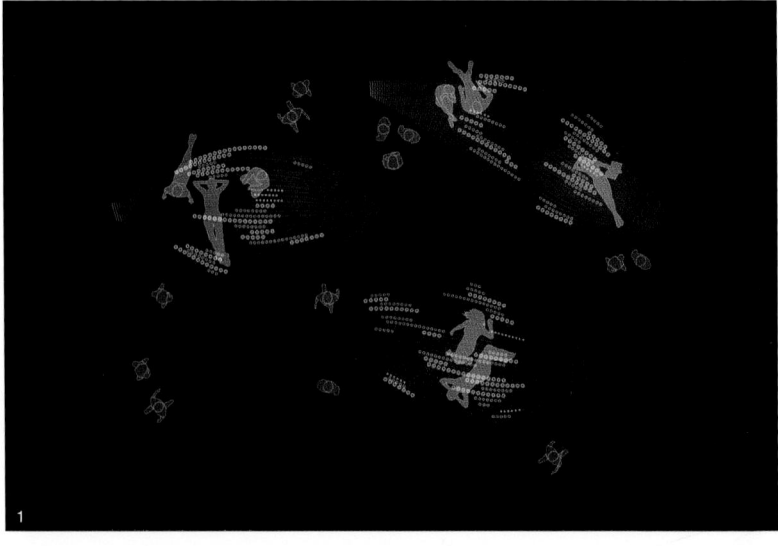

1

1: Users can position themselves within the various artificial microclimates created by the carpet.

2: Working prototype

3: Section

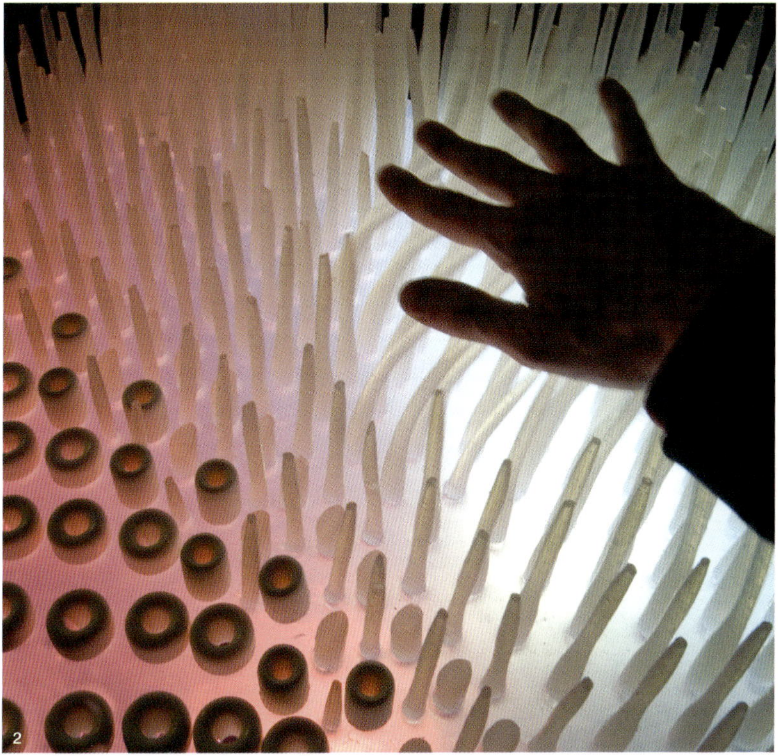

2

3

Wanderings

Installation and prototypes, Houston, Texas, 2008–9
with Benson Gillespie, Ned Dodington, Brian Shepherdson, Curt Gambetta,
and Viktor Ramos, with the support of the Rice School of Architecture

Wanderings tries to establish a climatic infrastructure for commercial and public
domains, taking existing variables and altering them to accommodate programmatic
activities. Looking for ways to lift materials out of dependence on surfaces and
services, Wanderings chooses to deploy them as building materials. It redefines
physical boundaries, and the resulting design innovation reaches to new spatial
and social organizations for the urban metropolis.

   The project does not seek to simply recondition exterior spaces to reproduce
familiar climates; rather, it seeks new territories of design, infrastructure, texture,
and social interaction. The intention is not only to move activities outside but also
to tease out new spatial and social implications when walls and geometry are no
longer defining factors.

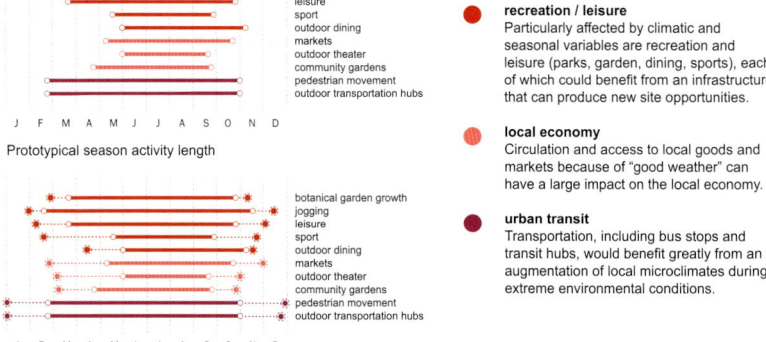

Prototypical season activity length

Seasonal expansion

● **recreation / leisure**
Particularly affected by climatic and
seasonal variables are recreation and
leisure (parks, garden, dining, sports), each
of which could benefit from an infrastructure
that can produce new site opportunities.

● **local economy**
Circulation and access to local goods and
markets because of "good weather" can
have a large impact on the local economy.

● **urban transit**
Transportation, including bus stops and
transit hubs, would benefit greatly from an
augmentation of local microclimates during
extreme environmental conditions.

1: Seasonal expansion
2–**3**: Filaments inside sealed air cavities
heat the seating and soil by conduction
and the surrounding air by convection.

4–9: Initial prototypes demonstrate the scale, materiality, lighting, and configuration of the shapes. Afterward, environmental tests will determine their suitability for augmenting and adapting existing microclimates.

10: Each unit may seem minimal in production, but collected together, they have the potential to make noticeable changes to local microclimates.

11: Unit detail

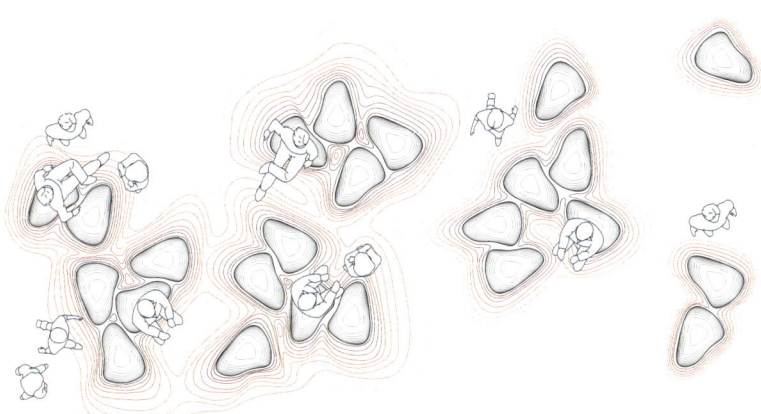

10

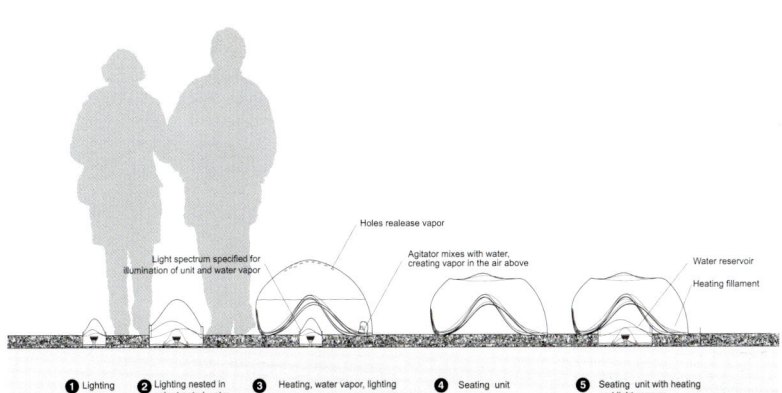

Light spectrum specified for illumination of unit and water vapor

Holes realease vapor

Agitator mixes with water, creating vapor in the air above

Water reservoir

Heating fillament

1 Lighting **2** Lighting nested in color treated water **3** Heating, water vapor, lighting **4** Seating unit **5** Seating unit with heating and light sources

11

Amplification

Installation, Los Angeles, California, 2006–7
as part of the Gen(h)ome Project

Temperature, light, and the scent and color of vegetation are usual considerations
when looking beyond pure architectural form to enhance the quality of domestic
spaces. Amplification proposes to use these qualities as design materials to explore
spatial relationships beyond tectonic geometries. The 17,500-square-foot
(1,625-square-meter) project is an intervention that heightens and manipulates
design material and energy often dismissed as too qualitative and unquantifiable
to visualize. In the Schindler House's courtyard and garden the intention was not
to build a new system, but instead to operate upon and amplify the design properties
of the existing location.

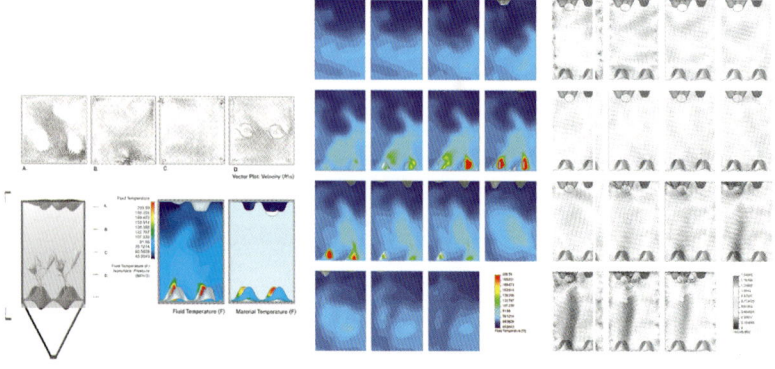

1

1: Software simulations using
computational fluid dynamics.
2: Site overview*

3: Each unit contained heating devices, fans,
water, and lighting, and was manipulated to
produce specifically designed conditions.*

4–9: Construction*
10: Fabrication components

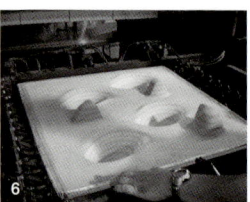

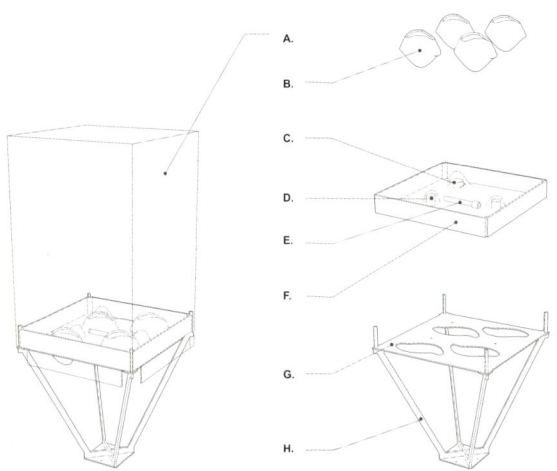

A. Acrylic Container
The container is engraved to trap water condensation on the interior in various sizes and patterns, trapping the water for recirculation.

B. Plant Containers
Serve as enclosures containing the vegetative planting medium and root systems.

C. Fans
Provide circulation and variation of air velocities within the system.

D. Lighting
2 MR 16 LED lights

E. Heaters
Four of the six latrines are equiped with artificial heating systems to control both water and air temperature, while two remaining latrines temperature are controlled only by existing environmental conditions.

F. PETG Plastic Water Basins
Tracer colors are added to water and subsequent condensation, creating visual and spatial boundaries.

G. Aluminum Structure

H. Steel Structure

11: Site aspect
photo credit: Joshua White

11

Asplund Library addition
One-stage competition, Stockholm, Sweden, 2006

This proposed addition to a library in Stockholm attempts to systematically organize and control exterior spaces as architecture. These spaces can be controlled and organized as systematically as interior spaces. Enlarging and exploiting the double-skin strategy of curtain walls, thermal heating is outwardly utilized to engage the surrounding site, interacting with artificial lighting and vegetation. The resulting spatial organization of the entrance, restaurant, and meeting centers can change in scale and intensity based on seasonal climate shifts.

The new library had unique programmatic requirements, including specified volumetric dimensions and climate control for book storage, administrative offices, and an auditorium, treating them as a form of poche to be accessed when needed. This is contrasted with more malleable amenities including a cafe, a restaurant, and public meeting areas. These spaces are defined and organized by amplifying material systems prevalent throughout the city and existing park where the library is situated, both engaging the site and extending its context beyond the property line.

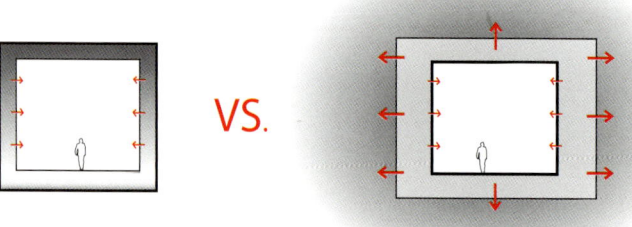

1

1: Skin system for mediating the interior
and skin system for exterior activation
2–**3**: Physical model

4: Physical model and thermal section

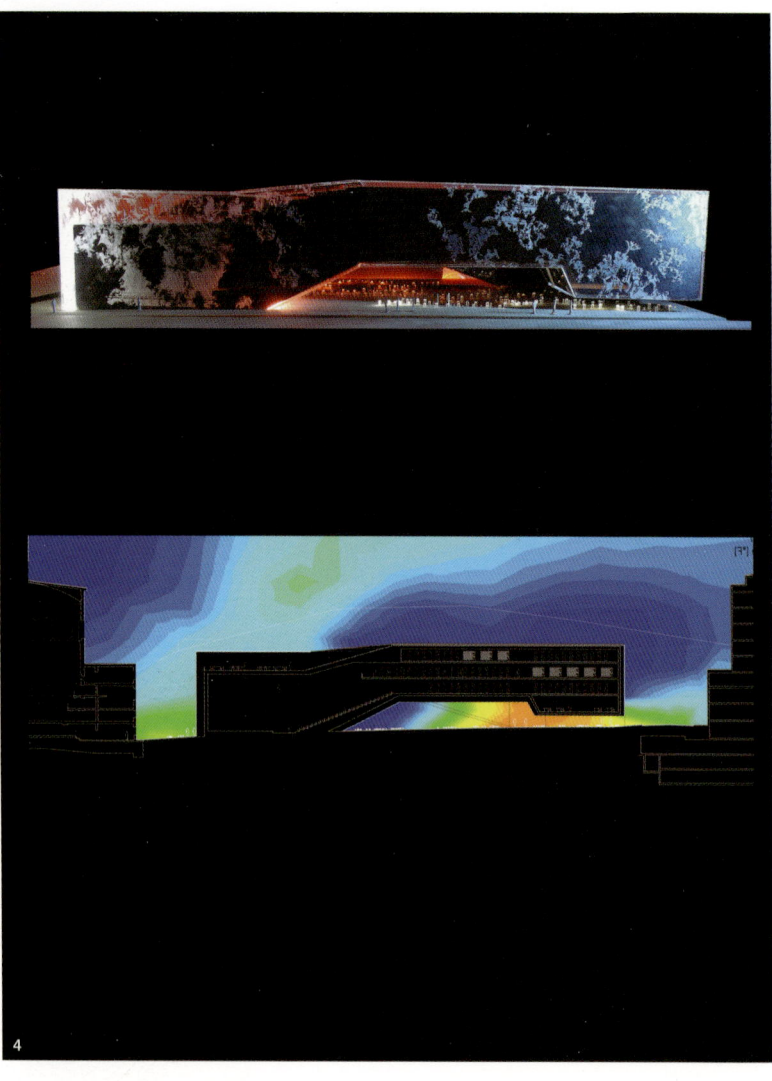

5: Site plan A (top) and B

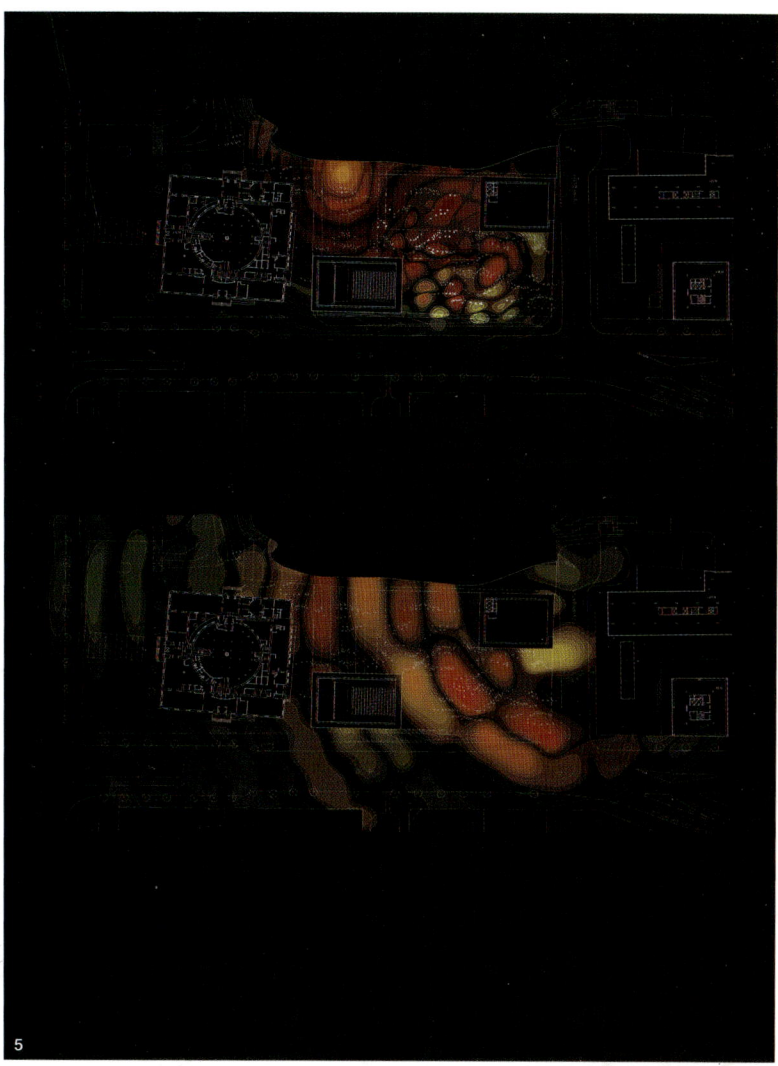

5